NAVIGATING THE TRENCHES

FAITH, FAILURE, AND FORTUNE IN REAL ESTATE

TRANSFORMING SETBACKS INTO
SUCCESS IN THE WORLD OF REAL ESTATE

COREY GRIFFIN

Navigating the Trenches Faith, Failure, and Fortune in Real Estate

Published by Elishia DuPree & Write Way Publishing

DEDICATION

To the warriors who walk through fire with faith as their shield.

To the ones who've been knocked down, counted out, and told they'd never make it—but kept going anyway.

To every soul who's stared at the minefield of life and whispered, "I'm stepping in anyway."

This book is for you.

To my wife, Nekiya—my partner, my anchor, my co-architect in this vision. Your love is the blueprint of everything I build.

To my children and grandchildren—may this book be a torch you carry into your own journeys. You are my legacy, my why, my forever motivation.

To my family, my community, and every person who believed in me when the world didn't—your faith lit the path when I couldn't see it.

And to the dreamers still standing at the edge of their own minefield: take the step. Even if your knees shake. Even if your voice trembles. Even if you've failed a thousand times before.

Because the first step isn't just the hardest—it's the most powerful.

CONTENTS

INTRODUCTION

Hey there, Awesome Reader!

Welcome to this wild ride of a book! Sit back, grab your favorite snack, and get ready to dive headfirst into a world of ideas that bubbled up, brewed, and transformed into what you hold in your hands. The genesis of this book was anything but ordinary. Picture this: late nights spent scribbling notes, countless cups of coffee fueling a frenzy of creativity, and an insatiable curiosity to understand the nuances of human experience that weave through the fabric of our daily lives. This isn't just a rehash of the same old tales; every word is packed with the vigor of exploration and a desire to share what I've learned along the way.

Believe it or not, the inspiration struck in the most unexpected of places—a bustling café, where the aroma of fresh pastries mixed with the sound of vibrant conversations sparked ideas that flickered in my mind like fireflies on a summer night. I realized the stories we live every day are laced with lessons just waiting to be unearthed. Every person you meet has a treasure trove of wisdom wrapped up in their unique experiences. Through rigorous research, engaging discussions, and plenty of soul-searching, I embarked on a quest to distill those narratives into insights that could resonate with you.

Now, let's talk about the nitty-gritty of the research process! I dove deep into books, articles, podcasts, and interviews, seeking a rainbow of perspectives to color the narrative I wanted to craft. Each piece of information, every snippet of dialogue, was a brushstroke in the masterpiece, which is this book. I pulled on threads from philosophy, psychology, and even a sprinkle of pop culture to create something that feels fresh and relatable yet deeply rooted in wisdom.

But that wasn't all—oh no, the adventure was just beginning! Through trial and error, I honed the structure of the book, ensuring that each chapter flows like a river, winding through the peaks and valleys of my thoughts and discoveries. I wanted to create a journey, not just a read, and that meant pacing it just right so you could savor every twist and turn. Each chapter builds on the last, layering in complexity and weaving a rich narrative that will hopefully leave you laughing, reflecting, and perhaps even a little shaken up.

As you embark on this journey, I encourage you to keep your heart and mind open. Let the ideas leap off the pages and dance into your consciousness. Don't be afraid to question, challenge, and explore what resonates with your own life experiences. This book isn't a dictatorship of ideas—it's more of an invitation to a meaningful dialogue. I want you to feel like you're sitting across from me over a cup of steaming cocoa, engaging in heartfelt conversations about life, love, and everything in between.

And hey, if you ever feel stuck or unsure, don't hesitate to revisit sections. Like the best friendships, the words within these pages can transform with time, give you new insights upon re-reading, and become even more valuable as you change and grow. Life is about evolution, and I hope this book will serve as a companion on your journey.

So, without further ado, let's dive in together! There are endless dimensions to explore, and I can't wait to hear how your perspective shifts along the way. This is not just my story; it's ours. Ready to turn the page and discover what awaits? Buckle up, it's going to be one exhilarating ride!

With bubbling excitement,
Corey Griffin

Chapter 1

THE FIRST STEP
INTO THE MINEFIELD

Understanding the Landscape

In the intricate world of real estate investing, understanding the landscape is pivotal to turning aspirations into accomplishments. The journey into this field often evokes a cocktail of excitement and trepidation. For many, it starts with the allure of the high-stakes environment filled with the promise of financial freedom and wealth accumulation. But behind that shimmering surface lies a complex network of cycles, property types, investment vehicles, and nuanced market conditions that can confound even seasoned investors. To thrive in this environment, one must be equipped with not just knowledge but also a keen sense of observation, analysis, and most importantly, faith and resilience.As we embark on this exploration, let's consider the story of "The Visionary Investor," an archetype within our narrative who successfully traversed this minefield. Their journey began with a thirst for knowledge and a burning desire to transform their financial trajectory. Eager yet apprehensive, they dove into books, attended seminars, and sought wisdom from mentors, all while grappling with moments of doubt. This subchapter will reflect on their initial encounters with market cycles, property types, and investment vehicles, weaving in statistical data and expert insights that expose the underlying patterns of the real estate landscape.Market cycles are perhaps one of the most critical aspects to grasp for any aspiring investor. The real estate market experiences fluctuations driven by various economic indicators, and understanding these cycles can significantly impact investment decisions. Economists typically identify four phases in the real estate market cycle: recovery, expansion, hyper-supply, and recession. Each phase presents unique opportunities and challenges.During the recovery phase, property values and rental rates begin to stabilize after a downturn. This period can attract investors eager to capitalize on low prices before a subsequent growth phase. The Visionary Investor recognized this early in their journey. In discussions with experienced players in the industry, they learned about the vast potential lying within distressed properties—those that require renovation or revitalization. The data supported what they heard: properties purchased during recovery tend to yield generous returns as the market shifts toward expansion. When the sphere transitions into the expansion phase, demand for housing and commercial space increases, and property values often rise. Investors who timed their entry correctly into this phase could see significant capital appreciation. However, it's essential to remain vigilant. Overzealous optimism can lead to risky bets, as evidenced by the real estate crash of the mid-2000s. The Visionary Investor observed how even seasoned investors could be swept up in the fervor, prompting critical reflections on the necessity of due diligence and market research.Treading cautiously, they began absorbing insights about hyper-supply, the stage when the market becomes oversaturated with properties. Here, the balance between supply and demand tips, often leading to price corrections. Understanding this phase is crucial; it's during hyper-supply that many inexperienced investors falter. An analysis of historical data reveals that markets experiencing hyper-supply often see rental vacancies rise, which can diminish cash flow for landlords. The Visionary Investor paid close attention to supply-demand ratios in their targeted markets, knowing that the right timing could mitigate risks.As market conditions shift into recession, it becomes imperative for investors to have a robust strategy. The Visionary Investor learned the importance of resilience during downturns, recognizing that while some investors frantically exited the market, others seized the chance to acquire undervalued assets. Statistics highlight that the real estate fortunes of a dwindling economy can create a fertile ground for those who possess the foresight and faith to withstand the uncertainty. Understanding the different property types is equally vital in navigating the landscape. Residential, commercial, industrial, and raw land investments each come with their own set of characteristics, risks, and rewards. The Visionary Investor initially focused on residential properties, drawn in by the simplicity of the market. After all, everyone needs a place to live. Investing in single-family homes and duplexes provided them a comfortable learning environment, with less complexity compared to commercial ventures. In immersing themselves in the statistics around residential real estate, they found that single-family homes tend to have lower volatility than other sectors. In a report from the National Association of Realtors, data indicated that home prices, while subject to fluctuations, remained relatively stable, especially in key urban areas. The Visionary Investor's analysis of historical price trends was revealing; neighborhoods undergoing regeneration often saw values soar, making them attractive targets for investment.Commercial real estate, while potentially more lucrative, presented the Visionary Investor with a steeper learning curve. Office buildings, retail spaces, and multi-family properties require an understanding of lease structures, tenant dynamics, and local business environments. In conversations with mentors, the Investor learned about the benefits of diversifying into commercial properties. Indeed, the data reflects that commercial real estate tends to outperform residential properties in terms of returns on investment over the long term. However, the initial hurdles of understanding complex rental agreements and navigating tenant relationships can be daunting.Industrial properties and raw land investments emerged as new possibilities, amplifying the Visionary Investor's understanding of market dynamics. While industrial real estate requires a grasp of logistics and manufacturing trends, raw land investments demand an understanding of zoning laws, environmental regulations, and potential development opportunities. Here, the power of strategic partnerships and networking within the industry became apparent. Surrounding oneself with experts who can provide insights in these specialized areas can bridge knowledge gaps.Equipped with knowledge of market cycles and property types, the Visionary Investor was ready to explore various investment vehicles. Each option—ranging from traditional direct ownership to real estate investment trusts (REITs) and crowdfunding platforms—comes with its own risk profile, benefits, and return expectations. Direct ownership, although potentially the most rewarding, also carries the weight of responsibility, including property management and maintenance. The Investor learned, through anecdotes shared by seasoned investors, how proper management can significantly influence cash flow and asset value. They noted the tales of those who delegated property management versus those who opted to self-manage. While self-management can save costs, it often demands a time commitment that many investors might not be prepared for.Real estate investment trusts (REITs) emerged as a more passive alternative. With a variety of specialized REITs dedicated to diverse property types, they can provide investors with exposure to various sectors without the pitfalls inherent to direct ownership. The Visionary Investor reviewed statistical data illuminating REIT performance over decades. They discovered how well-managed funds tended to offer dividends nearly rivaling stock returns while providing a hedge against inflation. Crowdfunding, the newcomer in the investment toolkit, appealed particularly to the Visionary Investor due to its potential for accessibility. This democratization of real estate investing opens doors for individuals who may lack the capital for large transactions. However, they also recognized the need for due diligence, understanding the risks associated with investment in new platforms and less established projects. The Visionary Investor's journey through the intricacies of real estate illuminated a crucial takeaway: the importance of consolidation and ongoing education. Each interaction, seminar, and real-life case study combined to form a larger picture of the market landscape. The stories of both success and failure provided them with valuable learning experiences, reaffirming their belief that setbacks are not just hurdles but integral pieces of the success puzzle. Throughout this process, statistical insights and expert opinions became pervasive threads that wove through their understanding of the real estate cycle. Industry reports and forecasts gained significance in shaping their expectations and decisions. They started to curate resources, forming a library of knowledge that would support their endeavors and allowing them to pivot and adapt in response to emerging trends. The ability to discern credible sources became another essential skill in navigating the landscape. In a world drenched in data, not all information holds equal weight. The Visionary Investor learned to differentiate between anecdotal advice and evidence-based insights, relying on reputable research firms, government statistics, and industry publications to inform their investment strategies. The lesson of focusing on what generates consistent, reliable returns remained central to their philosophy. Amidst the fluctuations and trends, the Visionary Investor came to appreciate the value of stable cash flow over speculative, high-risk investments. They realized that cultivating patience and a long-term perspective could yield tremendous benefits, allowing them to weather the inevitable storms of market volatility. As this subchapter draws to a close, it's clear that understanding the landscape of real estate is not simply about acquiring data; it's about cultivating a mindset of inquiry and adaptability. The path carved by the Visionary Investor illustrates how the interplay of market knowledge, investment strategies, and lessons drawn from both triumphs and setbacks can lead aspiring investors toward successful outcomes. Armed with an understanding of market cycles, property types, and investment vehicles—from the realms of residential homes to the complexities of commercial assets—the Visionary Investor has laid a solid foundation. This knowledge, paired with an unwavering belief in their ability to learn, adapt, and strategize, positions them to navigate the minefield of real estate with resilience and faith. Once again, the maxim remains clear: every setback is an opportunity, every failure a lesson. To emerge as successful investors, one must traverse through the trials, emerge steadfast, and apply the wisdom gleaned from experience and research. With faith and resilience, even the most arduous paths can lead to fortunes untold, propelling aspiring investors into the promising horizons of real estate success.

Mindset of a Successful Investor

The journey into the world of real estate investing is not merely a tactical maneuver; it's a psychological expedition. As aspiring investors stand on the precipice of opportunity, they must recognize that the foundation of their success is built upon a robust mindset. This chapter explores the mental preparedness required in the face of challenges, emphasizing the importance of resilience, optimism, and the ability to learn from setbacks. To illuminate this vital topic, we turn to insights gleaned from seasoned industry veterans and the wise words of 'The Mentor Sage,' a figure whose teachings transcend the trials of real estate to speak to the universal experience of striving for success in the face of adversity. In the interviews conducted with various real estate veterans, a common thread emerged: The most successful investors are those who view failure not as an endpoint but as a stepping stone towards growth. Each setback is a lesson, offering valuable insights that can propel future successes. For instance, one seasoned investor recounted a time when a major deal fell through at the last minute. Instead of wallowing in disappointment, he took a step back to analyze the situation. He found that the due diligence process had revealed significant issues with the property. This realization not only saved him from a financial pitfall but equipped him with the knowledge to avoid similar pitfalls in the future.'The Mentor Sage' teaches that the power of mindset cannot be overstated. He has often said, "In every failure, there is a seed of a greater success." This perspective requires a shift in how we approach challenges. Rather than viewing them as insurmountable obstacles, we must train ourselves to see them as opportunities for growth. Building this type of resilient mindset begins with self-awareness. Investors must learn to recognize their own emotional triggers when faced with setbacks. Perhaps it's the sting of rejection from lenders, or the frustration of a failed negotiation. Understanding these emotions allows investors to navigate them more effectively. One effective exercise for enhancing self-awareness is journaling. By writing down their thoughts and feelings during challenging times, investors can reflect on their emotional responses, identify patterns, and ultimately gain better control over their reactions.Optimism is closely intertwined with resilience. A positive outlook doesn't mean ignoring the realities of the market or the risks involved; instead, it's about maintaining hope and focus on the potential for success. Research has shown that optimistic individuals tend to set higher goals and are more persistent in pursuing them. To cultivate optimism, investors might practice gratitude daily. Reflecting on what went well, no matter how small, can create a more positive outlook on the investment journey and reinforce the belief that new opportunities lie ahead, even amidst difficulties.Another exercise that can enhance a resilient mindset involves visualization techniques. This practice is commonly employed by athletes to improve performance, but it is equally applicable to investors. By visualizing successful outcomes, whether it's closing a deal or launching a new property venture, investors can mentally prepare themselves for the challenges they will face. Visualizing scenarios, planning responses to potential setbacks, and envisioning the triumphant feelings that accompany success can build confidence and mental fortitude.Furthermore, establishing a growth mindset is crucial. Carol Dweck, a respected psychologist, categorizes mindsets into two main types: fixed and growth. Those with a fixed mindset believe their abilities are set in stone, while individuals with a growth mindset see their talents as malleable, improving through effort and learning. Successful investors actively embrace challenges, learn from criticism, and celebrate the success of others as a source of inspiration. Cultivating a growth mindset involves embracing the discomfort that comes with learning and viewing challenges as integral to personal and professional development.The narratives shared by experienced investors also emphasize the power of community. Surrounding oneself with a supportive network can foster a resilient mindset. This network, whether it consists of mentors, fellow investors, or even family and friends, provides encouragement during times of difficulty. Engaging in discussions about challenges and strategies fosters a sense of camaraderie and shared purpose. 'The Mentor Sage' often reminds us that "success is rarely a solitary endeavor." The highs and lows of real estate investment become more manageable when shared among a community of like-minded individuals who understand the journey.As we reflect on the mindset of a successful investor, we should also consider the role of continuous learning. The real estate landscape is ever-evolving, influenced by economic factors, technology, and consumer behavior. A commitment to lifelong learning allows investors to stay ahead of trends and adapt their strategies accordingly. Whether through formal education, networking with peers, or self-study, seeking knowledge equips investors to turn potential failures into informed decisions and successful outcomes.To facilitate this continuous learning, we encourage readers to create a personal development plan. This structured approach can include a combination of reading industry-related books, attending workshops, or engaging in online courses. Setting aside regular time for education encourages an active pursuit of growth and knowledge, strengthening the mental tools necessary to navigate the investment landscape.In conclusion, the mindset of a successful investor is a multifaceted assemblage of resilience, optimism, community, and a commitment to continuous learning. By consciously cultivating these attributes, aspiring investors can better prepare themselves for the minefields ahead. Every challenge faced is a potential catalyst for growth, a testament to the indomitable spirit of those who choose to invest in real estate.As you embark on your journey, remember the wisdom of 'The Mentor Sage:' "Success is not the absence of failure but the ability to rise and learn every time you fall." Embrace this mindset, and you will be equipped to transform setbacks into success, navigating the thrilling yet treacherous waters of real estate investment with confidence and purpose.

The Importance of Research

In the realm of real estate investing, where fortunes can be made or lost in the blink of an eye, the importance of diligent research cannot be overstated. For aspiring investors, the journey into this dynamic field can feel like stepping into a minefield. Every choice holds potential rewards and risks, making the ability to differentiate between the two essential for success. This subchapter aims to illuminate the critical role that thorough research plays in laying the groundwork for successful investments. Through the lens of 'The Resilient Newcomer,' readers will witness how undertaking diligent research transforms uncertainty into informed decisions.First and foremost, it's essential to recognize that real estate is not just about finding properties that appear attractive on the surface. It's about understanding the underlying factors that influence property values, rental markets, neighborhood dynamics, and economic conditions. Many beginners fall into the trap of superficial assessment, relying on aesthetics or anecdotes rather than employing a thorough analytical approach. By adopting a mindset of a proactive learner, aspiring investors can set themselves apart from those who merely dabble in the market.Take, for example, the story of Sarah, a hypothetical yet relatable figure we'll call 'The Resilient Newcomer.' When Sarah first decided to enter the world of real estate investing, she was filled with enthusiasm but also uncertainty. The prospect of buying her first investment property was daunting, and she could easily have succumbed to the allure of quick decisions based on market trends and flashy property listings. Instead, Sarah chose a different path. She dedicated considerable time to understanding the local real estate landscape.Sarah's journey began with market research. She scoured online real estate platforms, subscribed to industry newsletters, and followed local real estate agents on social media. She read industry reports that outlined trends in her chosen area, focusing on factors such as job growth, average income, population demographics, and historical price movements. What she discovered shocked her. While some neighborhoods were celebrated for their burgeoning development, others were facing economic challenges that could negatively impact her investment choices. Sarah learned that the true heart of real estate investment lies in the details, in understanding the dynamics at play.Armed with this knowledge, Sarah ranked neighborhoods not only on their current desirability but also on their potential for future growth. This critical analysis involved comparing crime statistics, school ratings, access to public transportation, and amenities like parks and shopping centers. Sarah understood that a desirable neighborhood could significantly impact her rental income and property appreciation over time. Through her meticulous research, she developed a comprehensive picture of each area, which informed her evaluation process.Once Sarah identified several neighborhoods that piqued her interest, she turned her focus to specific properties. Rather than relying solely on interest rates and the appeals of real estate agents, she delved into each property's financial feasibility. Understanding key metrics such as cash flow, return on investment (ROI), and capitalization rates played a vital role in her decision-making process. Sarah recognized the potential for properties to hold unforeseen costs, such as renovation requirements, property taxes, and management fees. By calculating these expenses upfront, she was better equipped to evaluate whether a property was truly a sound investment.To confidently navigate the numbers, Sarah adopted a systematic approach. She created a spreadsheet to compile data on potential properties. Each column represented a different factor: purchase price, estimated repair costs, expected rental income, and similar metrics. This transparency allowed her to compare properties side by side, identifying which ones posed viable investment opportunities and which ones were less favorable. Ultimately, Sarah's extensive research enabled her to develop a clear investment strategy that aligned with her financial goals.But research isn't merely about crunching numbers. It's about gathering information from diverse perspectives. Sarah knew that while online tools provided invaluable insights, firsthand experience holds tremendous weight. Thus, she prioritized connecting with local property managers, landlords, and tenants. She attended community meetings and forums, engaging with individuals who lived in the neighborhoods she was considering. This effort not only deepened her understanding of the community dynamics, but it also provided her with an intimate grasp of what renters wanted in a home.One of the discussions she attended highlighted a growing demand for short-term rental properties in her area due to an influx of tourists. Upon learning this, Sarah expanded her research to explore the feasibility of developing a property for that market niche. This level of determination and thoroughness set her apart from many newcomers who might have overlooked the value of community engagement. It's important to recognize that thriving as a real estate investor means accepting the need for continuous education and an adaptive approach. Even after purchasing her first property, Sarah continued to research and learn. She tracked market fluctuations and engaged with online communities to discuss trends and insights. As market landscapes inevitably change, staying informed ensures that investors can pivot effectively. However, in her journey, Sarah also faced numerous challenges. There were encounters with properties that, on the surface, seemed promising. Decked out with modern amenities and located in trending neighborhoods, they initially captivated her attention. Yet, upon conducting deeper research, she uncovered serious issues such as zoning violations or significant code infractions that would cost her significantly in the long run. The lesson here is profound: research is pivotal in safeguarding against future pitfalls; it can serve as a protective barrier against making snap decisions driven by excitement or fear of missing out.Moreover, Sarah learned the importance of building a strong network of professionals—real estate agents, contractors, appraisers, and lawyers—who could assist her in the research process. Each of these individuals brought their unique expertise to the table, providing her with insights that bolstered her understanding and, ultimately, her ability to make wise investment choices. By building relationships with these professionals, Sarah not only enriched her knowledge base but also established a support system that she could lean on in challenging times.As readers contemplate their own journeys, consider this: research can often feel like a daunting task. But taking the plunge into thorough investigation will yield rich rewards. It's impossible to overemphasize the impact of knowledge acquisition; with a well-invested foundation of knowledge, you can glean insights and perspectives that few amateur investors will possess. This kind of preparation differentiates those who merely tread water from those who swim confidently toward their financial goals.The results of Sarah's efforts speak for themselves. She successfully navigated her first investment, purchasing a multi-family unit in a neighborhood that had strong potential for appreciation. While others around her were still exploring possibilities, she was engrossed in her first tenant agreement. Sarah's ability to turn research into action demonstrated how critical it is to maintain that balance between knowledge and execution.Finally, it's essential for readers to recognize that research prepares you not just for the immediate investment but for a career in real estate as a whole. The skills you develop in assessing properties, understanding market dynamics, and networking with industry professionals serve as the backbone for continual growth. Just as Sarah experienced, the market will ebb and flow, and an investor's success is often tied to their willingness to adapt and evolve informed strategies.In conclusion, the story of 'The Resilient Newcomer' emphasizes that success in real estate investment begins with thorough research. It's the precursor to informed decisions, financial prudence, and lasting partnerships. By integrating the lessons learned from Sarah's journey, aspiring investors can transform their setbacks into success stories. Let faith and resilience guide you through this essential stage, and remember that in a field as competitive as real estate, knowledge is both the shield and the sword—equipping you to navigate the minefield with confidence and clarity. Embrace research, and let it be your compass as you embark on your real estate journey.

Chapter 2

FAITH AS A COMPASS

Navigating Doubt

D oubt is an insidious intruder. It creeps in during the quiet moments of a night spent strategizing over financial spreadsheets or blares in your ears during the high-pressure moments of negotiation. For many aspiring real estate investors, doubt can feel like an unwavering companion, whispering that the next deal might spell disaster, that past failures will repeat themselves, or that success is simply unattainable. This segment delves into these overwhelming feelings and how to navigate them, presenting the emotional narratives of 'The Resilient Newcomer' who bravely confronts and overcomes doubt on their journey to prosperity.Let's meet our Resilient Newcomer, Emily. Freshly out of college, Emily had always dreamt of becoming a real estate mogul. Equipped with a sharp mind, a small amount of savings, and her grandfather's old real estate books, she took her first tentative steps into the world of property investment. The thrill of possibilities coursed through her veins, but as her one and only property search began, so did the chorus of doubt.On her first outing to view potential properties, Emily gazed nervously at the decaying home on the corner of Maple Street. The shutters hung askew, and the yard was an overgrown mess—a far cry from the "fixer-upper" she'd envisioned. Her heart raced, not from excitement, but from a wave of self-doubt that washed over her. "What are you thinking? You can't renovate this place," a voice in her head echoed. Images of catastrophic investment haunted her thoughts. "You don't have the experience. You'll surely fail." As she stood before that house, it felt as if she had a choice, one that would set the course of her journey. She could succumb to that voice of defeat, retreat into safety, and continue her conventional nine-to-five job—or, she could muster a spark of faith and take the plunge. Fueled by her vision, the desire to rewrite the narrative of her life, and the righteous indignation that this would not be the end of her dream, she took her first step towards that house. Emily's story reflects the broader theme of navigating doubt in the pursuit of ambitious goals. Like many new investors, her inclination was to internalize her fears and, in doing so, stifle her faith. The journey to overcome doubt began not just with action, but with cultivating a mindset that fully acknowledged and confronted that doubt head-on. Personal affirmations became her lifeline. Every morning, Emily would stand in front of her bathroom mirror and repeat sentences that challenged her internal narrative: "I am capable of turning my dreams into reality." "Every successful investor has faced doubt; I'm no different." "I will learn from mistakes rather than be defined by them." These affirmations began to shift her internal dialogue. As she sat in her humble studio apartment, she started to write journal entries chronicling her journey— each filled with aspirations, fears, and reflections. On some particularly tough days, she would emphasize her emotional narratives about doubt. The lines would flow onto the page, structured and unfiltered: "I feel paralyzed by the weight of uncertainty. Every choice feels monumental and risks are daunting!" Yet, by parsing through these feelings, she embarked on a path of intentional self-reflection and honesty. Doubt, Emily learned, exists in tandem with ambition. It is the twin sister of aspiration that often hovers in shadows, lurking and waiting to pounce when the stakes are high. She realized it was vital to dismantle the raw, corrosive thoughts of self-doubt that weighed her down. Instead of viewing these fears as indicators of potential failure, she began to perceive them as signals—a necessary family member in the broader spectrum of her emotional state. Stories of those who have faced doubt yet persevered can serve as powerful motivators. Take the tale of Marc, another newcomer who encountered a similar struggle on his journey to real estate success. After his first two attempts to flip homes ended in financial losses, Marc was devastated. He questioned whether he was cut out for this business at all. Yet, amidst the despondency, he opened up to a community of fellow investors who served as a safe harbor during stormy waters. They shared their own stories of setbacks, reminding each other that failure isn't the end; it's merely a stepping stone toward growth. As Marc connected with others who had endured similar trials, his faith slowly shifted from a distant whisper to a loud and resounding mantra. He learned techniques to silence the negative chatter: visualization became a powerful practice for him. Whenever doubt crept in, he pictured himself in the final moment of victory, whether it was standing on a stage, sharing his story, or signing the paperwork to close a successful deal. Every vision of triumph further energized his resolve. For aspiring investors facing doubt, community support is paramount. Engaging with mentors, attending industry seminars, or joining local investment groups can cultivate an environment of shared experiences where doubt no longer feels isolating. It's easy to feel alone when uncertainty strikes, but building a supportive network can transform that fear into collective resilience. Emily and Marc both discovered the power of communal faith—that when one member of the group falters in belief, another stands ready to uplift them in faith. Another critical mental strategy to combat doubt is reframing negative thoughts. Instead of telling herself, "I will fail," Emily started rewording it to, "I may learn something valuable through this experience." This habit of positive reframing granted her permission to explore risk while lowering the personal stakes attached to any one failure. Real estate, she learned, is not about avoiding failure at all costs, but about being able to look at each setback through a lens of learning and growth. In real estate, every investor experiences discomfort; it actually serves as a sign of growth. The amount of uncertainty that defines the industry is staggering—market fluctuations, economic downturns, and changing tenant demands can all cause doubt to sprout like weeds. Emily drew strength from the concept of resilience, reorienting her perspective to see that discomfort can lead to growth. Every time she encountered a challenge, she would remind herself, "This is an opportunity to strengthen my problem-solving skills." Faith became her compass, guiding her through the dense fog of uncertainty. She meticulously charted her progress, marking milestones, however small, and celebrating those victories. Gratitude grew steadfastly alongside her faith. Each step that she took—whether it be learning about financing options or winning a negotiation—was a reminder that she was capable of so much more than she initially thought. It's essential to recognize that the process of navigating doubt is not linear; it will ebb and flow, often rising at the moments one might feel closest to their goals. Emily experienced this visceral surge of doubt when she received an offer on a property that she very much desired. Torn between excitement and fear, she reached a tipping point. Would accepting the offer mean a step toward fulfillment, or would it place her on the precipice of failure? The emotional tug-of-war distilled into one core question: did she have faith in her choices? In this vulnerable moment, she paused. Emily closed her eyes and took a deep breath. She remembered that faith didn't mean a lack of fear; it was the ability to act despite that fear. It meant that making educated decisions based on research rather than panic would serve her better. She also recalled the stories shared by her community friends, many of whom faced similar crossroads. Choosing to take that step meant she was willing to trust the process and put her values and skills to the test, regardless of the outcome. As the investor's journey unfolds, the melodies of doubt will always be part of the score. The key is not to eliminate all elements of doubt but rather to gain mastery over one's response to it. Rather than retreating in fear, one can stand firm with faith as an anchor. When one learns to navigate the internal storms of doubt with grace and resilience, obstacles become opportunities—and failures transform into stepping stones toward extraordinary successes. Ultimately, every successful investor speaks to the moments of fear and doubt that punctuated their success stories. They underscore the importance of persistence, utilizing strategies such as affirmations, community engagement, and resilience training to create an inner landscape rich with possibilities. For Emily, the transformation from doubt to determination became a powerful part of her journey—one that taught her that navigating uncertainty was, in fact, not the absence of doubt but the embrace of faith. With each property exploration, with every financial calculation, with every lesson learned, Emily began to embody her journey. Doubt became but a whisper, a reminder to persist. In the ebb and flow of her adventures in real estate, she forged a path illuminated by the unwavering faith that leads to genuine success. Each experience reinforced the principle that doubt is not the enemy; it is merely a stepping stone on the path toward greatness. It's this confluence of faith and resilience that will not only help you, dear reader, to navigate doubt but will also create a sturdy foundation upon which you can build your dreams. As you grapple with the uncertainties and challenge the doubts that arise in your pursuit of real estate investing, remember that faith is your compass, guiding you through every twist and turn. Lean into it, believe in your potential, and know that each setback is a setup for a comeback, a testament to the strength of your spirit. With faith as your unyielding ally, you, too, will transform doubt into an unwavering drive toward success.

Stories of Faith in Adversity

In the heart of the real estate journey, where uncertainty often looms like a dense fog, stories of faith and resilience emerge to illuminate the path. This subchapter intends to weave together the narratives of investors who encountered profound challenges on their journey. Through their experiences, we will explore how belief—often called "faith"—provided them with the motivation to navigate adversity and transform their setbacks into opportunities for growth.Many investors find themselves at a crossroads when their dreams encounter harsh realities. Yet, it is often during these moments of trial that the strength of faith becomes most evident. Let us dive into the stories of several investors who turned to their convictions in times of despair, finding not only hope but also an unyielding commitment to their goals.The first story is of a young woman named Eva. Just a year into her career as a real estate agent, she was filled with ambition. However, her first significant project—a mixed-use building in a neighborhood that was struggling to revitalize—would soon become a battleground. Initially filled with excitement, she faced a series of hurdles that would challenge her faith in herself and her dreams. The city council delayed permits for months, costs began to overrun, and she found herself grappling with unexpected construction issues that threatened to derail the project entirely.As anxiety began to close in, Eva turned inward. She sought solace in her faith, a practice she had grown up with but hadn't leaned on in recent years. Each morning she would journal her fears, asking for guidance. She reached out to mentors and formed a support network with fellow investors who had faced similar setbacks. These relationships were a lifeline, offering her both practical advice and emotional support.During a particularly dark night, when doubt threatened to extinguish her resolve, she attended a local community prayer circle. Surrounded by those who believed in a greater purpose, she felt renewed strength emerging from the collective intention of her peers. This gathering, grounded in faith, provided her the clarity needed to approach her challenges with creativity rather than despair.Eva's faith allowed her to reframe her situation. Instead of viewing each setback as a dead end, she began to see them as an opportunity to pivot and adapt her strategy. Her renewed perspective led her to negotiate more effectively with contractors, to seek alternative funding options, and to communicate transparently with investors about the project's challenges. Ultimately, her mixed-use building opened its doors to the community, becoming a symbol of resilience and the transformative power of faith in action.Another investor whose experience speaks volumes is Ron. A seasoned real estate entrepreneur, Ron faced what many would consider a career-threatening crisis. A high-stakes investment in a luxury apartment complex in a burgeoning city had initially shown promise. However, a sudden economic downturn resulted in rising vacancies, and Ron found himself struggling to keep the property afloat.The pressure only intensified as financial obligations piled up. The fear of failure loomed large. Yet, amidst the turmoil, Ron's faith, long practiced and deeply embedded in his values, began to guide him back to a place of clarity. He started each day with a commitment to prayer and reflection, seeking not just guidance for his business but for peace within his heart as well.Recognizing his isolation in the struggle, Ron reached out to his community for support. He began hosting weekly gatherings for local investors, fostering an environment where they could share struggles and successes openly. This practice did more than provide camaraderie; it ignited renewed hope. Ron discovered that others had also faced downturns, and many had flourished by evolving their approach. Inspired by their stories, he adapted his business model to prioritize the needs and preferences of potential tenants. He focused on creating a community-oriented environment that appealed to a diverse range of residents.Months later, as the apartments began to fill, Ron's initial challenge transformed into a thriving community hub. His faith in both his personal conviction and the collective strength of his peers turned a seemingly insurmountable obstacle into a story of triumph.The importance of community support in the face of adversity cannot be overstated. Often, the belief in oneself can feel tenuous; however, when coupled with the faith of others, it can create a powerful foundation for growth. This was exemplified in the story of Maria, an investor and mother of two who found herself juggling the demands of her family with the pursuit of her real estate ambitions. The pressure to succeed was compounded by the sudden loss of her husband, which thrust her into a world of uncertainty and grief.At first, Maria felt paralyzed by her circumstances. The thought of continuing in real estate felt overwhelming. However, with each passing day, she knew she had to muster the strength for her children—to provide not just financially but also emotionally. Deep down, she held onto a profound faith in her ability to create a better future. It wasn't about doing it alone; it was about finding and leaning on her community.She sought help from a local organization dedicated to supporting women in business. Through this network, Maria discovered a wealth of resources—mentorship, workshops, and connections to potential investors. Surrounded by women who had faced their own struggles, she found inspiration in their stories of perseverance. Together, they formed a supportive sisterhood; an unbreakable bond emerged, woven with the fabric of shared experiences and mutual encouragement.Maria would later say that it was the faith of these women that lifted her when she felt she could not stand. It ignited her own belief in her abilities, and she began to approach real estate with renewed vigor. Eager to find properties that provided safe and affordable housing for families, she shifted her focus to serve the community that had rallied around her in her time of need.As she navigated the complexities of her out-of-state investments, Maria relied on the new friendships she forged. These women became her sounding board, her team, and often, her family. It wasn't just her real estate portfolio that grew; it was her faith in life itself, her trust in the universe that things would eventually fall into place if she kept moving forward.The notion of faith and support is not limited to personal crises or tragedies. Even the most successful investors encounter market fluctuations—unexpected changes that can shake their foundations. Take James, for instance. He was a seasoned real estate mogul with a portfolio that spanned multiple states. His confidence was shaken when a significant market shift rendered several of his properties underperforming. At first, panic set in. The future seemed uncertain and his long-standing success felt threatened.James decided to take a step back, to breathe, and reflect on his journey. He immersed himself in discussions with his peers, many of whom had weathered similar storms. Through these conversations, he was reminded of the importance of adaptability. Leaning on his faith in resilience, he developed a strategy to diversify his portfolio, reallocating resources into emerging markets that were on the rise. His ability to pivot, bolstered by community insights and collective wisdom, allowed him to not only recover but to thrive.Perhaps what stands out most in each of these stories is not merely the triumph over adversity but the role that faith plays in transforming perspectives. Whether it is faith in a higher power, faith in oneself, or faith in others, it serves as an anchor during turbulent times. It is the thread that connects these narratives, illustrating that setbacks do not signify failure but serve as essential stepping stones toward eventual success.In sharing these stories, we create a tapestry of lived experiences to which future investors can relate. They reveal that while the journey in real estate is often fraught with challenges, it is equally rich with opportunities for personal growth, community connection, and the reaffirmation of one's beliefs. As aspiring investors read these accounts, may they find reassurance in the knowledge that adversity can be a catalyst for profound transformation, and that faith is the compass guiding them through the trenches. Ultimately, the journey of real estate investment is not just a financial odyssey; it is a deeply human experience. Through the stories of faith in adversity, we are reminded of the indomitable spirit within each of us—a spirit that shines brightest when faced with challenges, illuminating the path to success against all odds.

Chapter 3

FAILING FORWARD

Redefining Failure

The word "failure" often carries a heavy weight in our culture. It is associated with embarrassment, incompetence, and loss. This stigma can be especially pronounced in high-stakes fields like real estate, where every investment is scrutinized, and every misstep can potentially lead to financial ruin. However, as we delve into the world of real estate investing, it becomes clear that failure is not only inevitable but also an invaluable teacher. In this subchapter, we will confront the traditionally negative perception of failure head-on and explore how it can be redefined as a crucial stepping stone towards success.In using the allegory of transformation, we look towards a prominent figure in the real estate industry, known affectionately as "The Real Estate Tycoon." This individual, having forged a successful career spanning decades, has encountered their share of mishaps and setbacks. Through interviews and case studies, we will uncover the turning points in their journey—moments that could have easily spelled disaster but instead served as the groundwork for remarkable comebacks.One of the most poignant stories shared by The Real Estate Tycoon involves their first foray into commercial real estate—a venture that seemed promising on paper. With meticulous planning and a substantial investment, they acquired a dilapidated office building in an up-and-coming neighborhood. Initial projections showed high potential returns, and everyone around them was optimistic. However, what ensued was a series of unforeseen challenges that would test not only their business acumen but also their resolve. The building, once believed to be a hidden gem, revealed its true nature—a construction nightmare. From leaky roofs to outdated electrical systems, the issues seemed to compound weekly. As costs mounted, The Real Estate Tycoon watched their projected profits dwindle into the abyss. Anxiety began to overshadow their enthusiasm, and self-doubt crept in. Was this the moment that would define their career? As they navigated the challenges, it became evident that they were at a critical junction: succumb to the failure or rise above it. In what could have been a dramatic collapse, The Real Estate Tycoon chose to redefine their perception of failure. Instead of wallowing in the setbacks, they took a step back to assess the situation holistically. They realized that every failed aspect of the renovation was a lesson in disguise. For instance, they reached out to industry professionals for guidance. Through frank conversations, they discovered that many had encountered similar hurdles and came out stronger on the other side. This sense of community helped shift their perspective, transforming isolation into collaboration. Next, they adopted a principles-based approach to problem-solving. Instead of letting emotions govern their decisions, they began to cultivate a mindset rooted in resilience and adaptability. The Tycoon approached their challenges with curiosity rather than fear. They immersed themselves in learning, reading about successful real estate entrepreneurs who had faced adversity and emerged triumphant. This newfound knowledge became their toolkit, equipping them to tackle the issues with informed strategies. The turning point came when The Real Estate Tycoon decided to evolve their financial strategy. Rather than relying solely on their initial investment, they explored alternative financing options. This included seeking partnerships with established investors who could inject capital into the project, as well as exploring crowdfunding avenues. By leveraging others' strengths and resources, they transformed a seemingly disastrous project into a collaborative venture full of potential. The building that once felt like an anchor became a shared mission. The turnaround wasn't instantaneous. It required grit, unwavering faith, and an ongoing commitment to learning. Renovations took longer than expected, and unexpected costs continued to arise. Each hurdle became an opportunity for refinement. Failure, instead of being a destination, became part of the journey. Over time, the building was revitalized. What had started as a daunting failure turned into a multifaceted success story, culminating in a thriving rental property that generated income beyond the initial projections. Beyond the financial success, The Real Estate Tycoon embraced the personal growth that stemmed from the experience. They emerged not only as a more knowledgeable investor but also as a mentor for those who would come after them. The lessons learned from failures serve as foundational pillars upon which one can build an enduring legacy. The stigma surrounding failure often undermines ambition and the drive to take risks. However, by reframing our understanding of failure from a negative endpoint to a valuable tool for learning, investors can adopt a more courageous approach to real estate. The case of The Real Estate Tycoon is not an isolated incident. Many renowned figures in the industry—people like Barbara Corcoran and Donald Trump—have faced their share of failures and obstacles. Barbara Corcoran famously stated that she learned more from her failures than her successes, emphasizing that failure is merely a step towards building something greater. This shared narrative among successful individuals highlights a universal truth: failure is woven into the fabric of success. Each setback provides insight into our strategies, forces us to ask critical questions, and unveils areas where we can grow. Moreover, understanding this fact can engender a sense of resilience among aspiring real estate investors, helping them cultivate a mindset that embraces rather than fears failure. To embody this redefined mindset, there are various strategies that can assist budding investors. First and foremost, it is essential to shift internal dialogue. Instead of thinking, "I failed," consider rephrasing it to, "I learned." Language shapes perception, and altering how we speak about failure can lead to a transformative mindset.Another strategy is to frame failure as a rite of passage. Drawing upon stories from experienced investors can illustrate how common setbacks are in the industry. By realizing that failure is an inherent part of any entrepreneur's journey, investors may find a sense of camaraderie and motivation, rather than isolation.Furthermore, aspiring real estate investors should actively seek mentorship. Stories of perseverance from seasoned professionals serve to cultivate an environment where failure is normalized as part of the learning process. Mentors can provide critical insights from their own experiences and encourage investors to push through challenging times, armed with newfound knowledge and perspective. Celebration of milestones, no matter how small, is also crucial. Every step taken—every lesson learned—should be acknowledged. By celebrating progress, individuals can maintain motivation and reinforce the notion that setbacks are merely temporary.In conclusion, the journey of real estate investment is fraught with challenges, and setbacks are inevitable. However, by redefining failure, one can significantly enhance not only their professional endeavors but their personal growth as well. The story of The Real Estate Tycoon serves as a testament to the transformative power of resilience and learning. As aspiring investors embrace failure as a stepping stone to success rather than a stumbling block, they pave the way for a future that is not only rich in opportunity but also grounded in the wisdom gained through experience. This is the essence of failing forward—transforming setbacks into success and embedding faith in the journey.

Lessons Learned

In the world of real estate investing, failure is not just an inevitable part of the journey; it is a crucial part of your education. Each flop, misstep, and detour is a stepping stone toward becoming a more successful and resilient investor. The challenge lies in not being overwhelmed by the negative emotions that often accompany failure but rather in observing, learning, and growing from these experiences. Keeping a journal to document your failures and the lessons you glean from them serves as an essential tool in transforming setbacks into opportunities for growth. The journey of 'The Visionary Investor' is an illustration of how one can intentionally analyze failures to extract invaluable lessons. This journey starts with the understanding that every failure has a story. Instead of viewing a failed investment as a mere blemish on your track record, approach it as a rich tapestry of experience waiting to be unraveled. Begin your journaling practice by dedicating a page to each failed investment or venture. Write down the details: what was the property type, where it was located, the purchase price, and the anticipated returns. Next, delve deeper into your decision-making process. What was your rationale for investing in this property? What factors seemed favorable at the time of purchase, and what blind spots did you overlook? By capturing these initial intuitions and analysis, you establish a baseline from which you can gauge your growth over time. After documenting the specifics of the investment, reflect on the results. How did the operational realities differ from your expectations? What key decisions led you astray, and were there aspects that you indeed executed well? This reflection phase is crucial. As you walk through your past decisions, you'll likely notice recurring themes, tendencies, or emotional responses that affect your judgment. Perhaps you rushed into an investment due to peer pressure or convinced yourself of a property's potential because it aligned with your personal aspirations rather than the actual market data. One of the key lessons learned from failure is the importance of due diligence. This concept is often thrown around in real estate circles, but what does it genuinely mean in practice? For 'The Visionary Investor,' due diligence entails more than just basic research. It is about deeply understanding market trends, the socio-economic backdrop of the investment location, and the financial implications of every minor detail in your deal. As you chronicle your journey, take stock of the research methodologies you used. Did you rely solely on third-party reports, or did you also engage in grassroots research by connecting with local communities, inspecting properties personally, or leveraging your network for on-the-ground insights? Consider a failure that 'The Visionary Investor' encountered while investing in a multifamily property. Initial numbers suggested promising cash flow prospects, but after purchasing, drastic fluctuations in the rental market eroded anticipated returns. Upon reflection, they discovered that peer insights had led them to overlook neighborhood developments that would impact rent prices. In their journal, they documented the significance of comprehensive market analysis, emphasizing the importance of examining current trends while anticipating potential shifts. This newfound understanding became a cornerstone of their future investment decisions. Another vital lesson learned is the art of patience and timing. Real estate is as much about timing as it is about opportunity. 'The Visionary Investor' often operated under the assumption that acting quickly would grant a competitive edge. However, some of these impulsive decisions led to costly mistakes. By reflecting on these failures, they began to recognize the power of patience—understanding that waiting for the right opportunity, thoroughly assessing all risks, and allowing time for further research ultimately built a stronger foundation for success. As you document your failures, take note of your emotional responses throughout the process. How did you feel during the initial excitement of finding a property? Did fear dictate your decisions when challenges emerged? Understanding your emotional landscape can be just as important as grasping the technical aspects of real estate investing because our emotions can cloud our judgment. 'The Visionary Investor' learned that embracing a mindset of resilience—where each setback became a lesson rather than a defeat—transformed their trajectory. They began to see hurdles as badges of honor, reflections of their tenacity rather than evidence of their shortcomings. To enhance your journaling practice, consider adding a 'lessons learned' section to each entry. What have you discovered about yourself as an investor through this failure? Which strategies could you try differently next time? Reflecting on these insights allows for continuous improvement. It ensures that your failures do not exist in isolation—they become stepping stones toward a seasoned investment strategy. In addition to the personal journey, draw inspiration from stories of other investors. 'The Visionary Investor' found motivation in the tales of others who faced failures before achieving significant successes. Hearing these stories helped contextualize their journey and understand that setbacks are not a personal failure but a universal experience among those pursuing ambitious goals. For each lesson you pen down, draw parallels with these stories of resilience and determination. As you journal, create actionable steps to integrate these learned lessons into your future investment strategies. Set specific, measurable, attainable, relevant, and time-bound (SMART) goals based on your reflections. If due diligence has been a recurring theme in your failures, for example, commit to a more robust research plan for your next potential investment. Perhaps this means allocating time to meet with an industry expert or attending workshops on market analysis. By transforming lessons learned into concrete actions, you create a pathway to not only avoiding past mistakes but also demonstrating growth in your investing acumen.Networking can also serve as a valuable resource in extracting lessons from failure. Engage with fellow investors, joining forums or local meetups where stories of loss and resilience are shared. Sharing your own experiences can be cathartic and insightful, while also providing opportunities to learn from the challenges others faced. Hearing varying perspectives on common pitfalls cultivates a rich dialogue around failure, fostering a community of supportive investors who can help one another navigate their journeys and keep each other accountable. The journey of 'The Visionary Investor' teaches that documenting failures is more than a therapeutic practice; it's a powerful tool for transformation. Each encounter with failure is a lesson waiting to be captured, analyzed, and eventually applied. With every positive action that results from a failure, you cultivate not just a measurement of success through your journal but tangible growth as an investor. As you embark on this reflective practice, remember that faith plays a crucial role in your journey. Faith in yourself, your abilities, and the notion that each setback can illuminate a path toward success will sustain you through even the toughest times. Incorporating a spiritual or philosophical angle into your journaling may be beneficial. Whether you connect with scriptures, motivational quotes, or personal mantras, these elements can fortify your mindset, reminding you that resilience in the face of adversity is a core tenet of successful investing.As you compile your journals over time, take moments to revisit your earlier entries. Track your evolution as both a person and an investor. What patterns have emerged? How have your strategies shifted? Which mindsets or beliefs no longer serve you? Monitoring your growth fosters a sense of accountability and keeps the lessons learned at the forefront of your journey. In conclusion, the act of journaling provides a robust framework for extracting lessons from the failures that are often the most educational chapters of your investment journey. It is not merely about recording experiences but rather about reflecting, learning, and growing from them to pave the way for future successes. Embrace your struggles; they are the very fabric of your investment narrative. Through the journey of the 'The Visionary Investor,' let their story inspire you to transform your failures into powerful lessons that inform your every decision, fortifying your faith and resilience as you navigate the ever-changing landscape of real estate investing.

Embracing the Growth Mindset

Embracing the Growth MindsetThe journey into the realm of real estate investment is often punctuated by obstacles and setbacks. To navigate these challenges effectively, it is essential first to cultivate a growth mindset. This concept, popularized by psychologist Carol Dweck, revolves around the belief that abilities and intelligence can be developed through dedication, hard work, and resilience. Embracing this mindset not only empowers investors to view failures as stepping stones toward their goals but also fosters an enduring commitment to personal and professional growth. When faced with adversity, many individuals instinctively adopt a fixed mindset, perceiving challenges as insurmountable barriers. Conversely, those who embody a growth mindset see these same hurdles as valuable opportunities for learning and improvement. This subchapter will explore the critical components of the growth mindset, provide actionable strategies to cultivate it, and share inspiring anecdotes from seasoned investors who have turned obstacles into accomplishments.To truly understand the power of a growth mindset, it is essential to first delve into its foundational principles. At its core, a growth mindset hinges on the belief that intelligence and talent are not static traits, but rather capacities that can be developed. This perspective not only enhances motivation but also fosters resilience. It encourages individuals to embrace failure as part of the learning process, ultimately leading them to greater success in their endeavors.For aspiring real estate investors, the ability to view failures as opportunities is paramount. The real estate market is notoriously unpredictable, and it is all too easy to become disheartened after a failed deal or a poor investment choice. However, cultivating a growth mindset equips investors with the resilience to bounce back and learn from setbacks. For instance, consider the story of Sarah, a young investor who faced a significant loss on her first property. Rather than allowing disappointment to deter her, she took the time to analyze her mistakes, seeking feedback from mentors and peers. Through this process, she not only discovered valuable insights about market trends but also developed a newfound appreciation for her own capacity to adapt and grow. Sarah's experience exemplifies the transformative power of a growth mindset, which enabled her to turn failure into a foundational lesson for future success. The next step is to implement strategies that nurture and strengthen a growth mindset. One effective technique is reframing failure. Instead of viewing a setback as a definitive end, see it as a catalyst for growth. This shift in perspective can drastically alter one's response to challenges. For instance, if an investment does not yield the expected returns, rather than dwelling on the loss, investors should assess what went wrong and what can be learned from the experience. Questions to consider include: What could I have done differently? What market indicators did I overlook? This analytical approach not only fosters a more resilient mindset but also encourages continuous learning. Another valuable strategy is to surround oneself with a supportive network. Engaging with like-minded individuals who embrace the growth mindset can have a profound impact on one's own perspective. Seek out mentors, attend workshops, or join investment groups where sharing experiences is encouraged. The exchanges within these networks can serve as powerful reminders that everyone encounters failures, but those who persist and learn are the ones who ultimately succeed. Additionally, practicing self-compassion is crucial in developing a growth mindset. It is essential to recognize that failure is not a reflection of one's worth, but rather a natural aspect of the journey. Self-criticism can inhibit growth and lead to fear of trying again. By replacing self-judgment with self-encouragement, investors can create an internal environment that is conducive to experimentation and risk-taking. Techniques such as mindfulness meditation can help cultivate this self-compassion, allowing investors to approach their challenges with a more accepting attitude. Furthermore, setting specific, achievable goals can empower investors to stay focused on growth. Rather than viewing success as a distant aspiration, break it down into manageable milestones that can be achieved over time.

Celebrate small wins along the way to maintain motivation and reinforce the belief that progress is possible. For example, if your goal is to purchase a property, set interim goals such as researching neighborhoods, building a network of real estate agents, or attending open houses. Each completed goal serves as a testament to your capabilities and dedication to growth. An essential aspect of embracing a growth mindset is cultivating an attitude of curiosity. Instead of approaching real estate challenges with a sense of dread or resignation, allow curiosity to guide your exploration. Ask questions, seek knowledge, and pursue new perspectives. This mindset encourages investors to view every challenge as a chance to gain insights and refine their strategies. Engaging with books, podcasts, and seminars can expand one's understanding and spark innovative ideas for overcoming obstacles. In addition, embracing constructive feedback is a powerful tool for developing a growth mindset. Rather than shying away from criticism or seeing it as a personal affront, approach feedback as a valuable opportunity for growth. Whether it comes from partners, mentors, or clients, constructive criticism can illuminate blind spots and reveal areas for improvement. Developing the ability to receive feedback graciously and to implement it effectively can elevate an investor's capabilities and strategies significantly. To illustrate the impact of a growth mindset further, let us examine the journey of James, a seasoned investor who faced years of fluctuating markets and equally challenging failures. Early on, James experienced a series of unfortunate investments that led to significant financial losses. Rather than resigning himself to a cycle of defeat, he chose to embrace the setbacks as invaluable life lessons. He meticulously documented the attributes of each failed investment and created a framework for analysis. Over the years, James transformed his failures into a robust strategy that propelled him to success in the market. His ability to embrace the lessons learned from his early missteps showcased the real power of a growth mindset, as it allowed him to refine his approach and emerge stronger. As we delve deeper into the importance of maintaining a growth mindset, it is crucial to recognize the role of resilience in the face of adversity. Resilience is not simply about enduring hardship; it is about rising from it with newfound strength and insight. In the context of real estate investing, resilience equips individuals with the fortitude to persevere through periods of difficulty. It enables investors to remain flexible, adapt to changing market conditions, and continuously refine their strategies. Equipping oneself with resilience is akin to building mental and emotional muscles. Just as physical strength is developed through training and practice, resilience flourishes when one consistently embraces challenges and seeks growth. Techniques to enhance resilience include developing a solid support system, engaging in physical activity, practicing gratitude, and reframing negative self-talk into encouraging affirmations. The story of Maria illustrates resilience beautifully. After encountering a significant financial loss due to unforeseen market changes, she initially struggled to accept the reality of her situation. However, she used the experience as an opportunity to rebuild her strategy, reevaluate her financial goals, and seek outside support. By constructing a network of fellow investors and mentors, she gained not only a sense of community but invaluable resources and encouragement. Over time, Maria emerged from her setback with renewed vigor, successfully secured additional properties, and transformed her initial loss into a wellspring of growth and opportunity.Ultimately, cultivating a growth mindset requires intentional practice and commitment. It necessitates an ongoing dedication to self-improvement, curiosity, and empathy. As aspiring investors navigate the complexities and uncertainties of real estate, the principles of a growth mindset will be instrumental in shaping their journey toward success. By embracing challenges, reframing failures, and leaning on supportive networks, aspiring investors can foster resilience and create opportunities for growth. Importantly, the journey toward evolving a growth mindset is ongoing. It is not a destination but a continuous process that demands awareness and proactive engagement. Regularly reflecting on one's experiences can deepen the understanding of personal growth, allowing for adjustments and refinements along the way. As you embark on your journey in the world of real estate investment, remember that every setback can serve as a powerful catalyst for growth. The ability to embrace challenges, cultivate resilience, and maintain a growth mindset will not only redefine your approach to investment but will also lay the foundation for a rewarding and fulfilling career. With faith in your abilities and a commitment to personal growth, you will find that the trenches of real estate are not mere obstacles to overcome but rich grounds for transformational success. In this ever-evolving landscape, your growth mindset will serve as a guiding beacon, illuminating the path toward a prosperous future.

Chapter 4

THE RESILIENCE FACTOR

Building Psychological Armor

Building Psychological ArmorIn the world of real estate investing, setbacks and failures are an inevitable part of the journey. The market can be unpredictable, and no amount of research or planning can eliminate that uncertainty. This is where resilience becomes not just a beneficial trait, but a crucial component of success. The psychological armor we build protects us against the harsh realities of each misstep, providing the fortitude required to recalibrate and move forward. This subchapter aims to unpack the elements of resilience necessary in real estate investing and illustrate their significance through real-life examples, including insights from "The Resilient Newcomer." Understanding resilience begins with recognizing that it is not merely an innate characteristic but a skill that can be cultivated. Like any other skill, resilience involves deliberate practice and a commitment to personal growth. Investors face an array of challenges, from market fluctuations to tenant issues, each demanding a mindset that embraces adaptability and nurtures perseverance. The stories of successful real estate investors serve as vital lessons, illustrating how faith and resilience are integral to navigating the often-turbulent waters of this industry. The journey of the resilient newcomer is particularly telling. Consider the case of Maria, a self-taught investor who entered the market during a downturn. Facing initial struggles from a lack of capital and unfavorable market conditions, Maria realized that her success would depend on her ability to manage stress and maintain her focus. Through her journey, she learned to cultivate self-care routines that became her foundation during trying times. By prioritizing her mental and emotional well-being, Maria found the strength to pivot her strategies and adapt to the evolving landscape of real estate. The significance of self-care cannot be overstated. In the midst of overwhelming stress, our mental clarity can become clouded, making it challenging to make sound decisions. Maria developed a self-care regimen that included regular exercise, mindfulness practices, and scheduling breaks to prevent burnout. Each of these practices contributed to a more resilient mindset, allowing her to approach setbacks with a clear head. By prioritizing her well-being, Maria found that she was not only more motivated but also more equipped to face challenges head-on. Stress management is also a critical part of building psychological armor. Every investor, regardless of their experience level, encounters stress. For seasoned investors, the stakes can be exceptionally high, while newcomers may feel overwhelmed by the learning curve. In the case of Maria, she grappled with stress by adopting an approach rooted in mindfulness and perspective shifts. She learned to view challenges not as insurmountable obstacles but as opportunities for growth and learning. This mindset allowed her to reframe her narrative—an important step in fostering resilience. A powerful technique Maria employed involved visualizing her challenges as a story unfolding rather than a series of failures. When a potential deal fell through or a market downturn affected her investments, instead of succumbing to despair, she focused on the lessons hidden within each experience. Visualization techniques like this empower investors to manage their emotional responses, encouraging them to take action rather than retreating in fear. Another cornerstone of resilience lies in maintaining focus during turbulent times. Real estate investing is rife with distractions—not only from the ever-fluctuating market but also from personal uncertainties and external pressures. Maria discovered that by creating a structured routine that included goal-setting and time blocking, she could maintain focus on her overarching objectives. This approach enabled her to chip away at her ambitions bit by bit, transforming seemingly insurmountable goals into manageable tasks.In her pursuit of resilience, Maria established a clear vision for her future. She crafted a comprehensive business plan, clearly outlining her goals and the steps necessary to achieve them. This plan became her guiding light, particularly during challenging times when doubt threatened to creep in. By regularly revisiting and refining her vision, she fortified her psychological armor, ensuring that she remained anchored even when external circumstances shifted.The importance of community support should not be underestimated in the context of resilience. Surrounding oneself with a network of supportive peers provides an additional layer of psychological protection. For Maria, this meant seeking out fellow investors who understood the unique stresses and pressures of the real estate world. Mentorship played a significant role as well, with experienced investors offering guidance, encouragement, and occasional reality checks. The collective wisdom of a community fosters resilience not only through shared knowledge but also through emotional encouragement.Investors also need to cultivate a fearlessness in the face of risk. The fear of failure can paralyze even the most ambitious investors, preventing them from taking the steps necessary to succeed. Maria tackled this fear by embracing a mindset that welcomed experimentation. She viewed each investment decision as a learning opportunity, whether or not it resulted in financial gain. This perspective freed her from the fear of making mistakes, allowing her to navigate the complexities of the market with confidence.A critical lesson learned from "The Resilient Newcomer" is the power of perseverance. Resilience goes hand in hand with grit—the determination to keep pushing forward despite setbacks. Maria's journey is replete with instances where perseverance became her greatest ally. Each setback became a stepping stone for growth, and each challenge reinforced her commitment to her goals. This development of grit prepares investors not just to weather the storm, but to emerge stronger on the other side.One of the most profound techniques that Maria and many successful investors employ is the practice of gratitude. In challenging times, when negativity threatens to overwhelm, focusing on the positive aspects of their journey fosters resilience. Maria kept a gratitude journal, jotting down lessons learned, relationships built, and moments of success, no matter how small. This habit shifted her focus from what went wrong, to what was going right, imbuing her with the strength to push through adversity.Additionally, the act of continuous learning feeds into resilience. Investors must remain adaptable in a market that changes daily. By embracing continuous education—whether through formal coursework, webinars, or reading—investors expand their knowledge and skillset. Maria found that her intentional investment in learning not only built her confidence but also provided her with new strategies for overcoming market challenges.As she navigated her way through various market shifts, Maria discovered that resilience is as much about mindset as it is about action. Those who possess a growth mindset tend to embrace challenges as opportunities and are more likely to bounce back quickly from setbacks. By cultivating a growth mindset, real estate investors expand their capacity for resilience, transforming potential failure into powerful lessons.In conclusion, building psychological armor in real estate investing is a multifaceted process. Through self-care, stress management, community support, and a commitment to learning, investors can cultivate resilience. The journey of the resilient newcomer serves as a valuable reminder that setbacks are not the end of the road but rather an integral part of a much larger journey. Resilience is not merely about survival; it's the bedrock upon which success can be achieved. Embracing this mindset equips investors to rise above turmoil and emerge stronger, inspiring those around them to do the same. Faith and resilience are not just concepts to be understood; they are the guiding principles that, when practiced, enable us not only to navigate the trenches of real estate investing but to triumph in the end. By honing these qualities, we can face an unpredictable future with confidence, transforming adversity into a foundation for lasting success.

Stories of Resilience

In the world of real estate, the path to success is seldom a straight line. Rather, it is a winding road filled with unexpected bends, steep climbs, and occasional detours. The stories we share in this subchapter highlight the resilience essential for overcoming the challenges that often accompany real estate investments. These narratives showcase tenacious investors who faced adversity head-on, turned failures into valuable lessons, and ultimately carved out their paths to success.One such story is that of Maria Torres, an aspiring real estate investor who entered the market during one of the most challenging economic downturns in recent history. When Maria decided to pivot from her corporate job to real estate, she was filled with hope and ambition. She meticulously researched the market, found a promising condo in a neighborhood on the verge of revitalization, and confidently submitted her offer. However, what Maria initially thought would be her breakthrough investment soon turned into a nightmare.After closing on the property, things began to unravel. The condo, which had seemed pristine during the viewing, was riddled with hidden problems. Plumbing issues emerged, the roof leaked, and the anticipated tenant market in the area failed to materialize as planned. Overwhelmed by mounting repair costs and a lack of rental income, Maria felt as though her dream had quickly turned into a nightmare. With her savings depleting and uncertainty looming, she nearly gave up.Yet instead of throwing in the towel, Maria leaned into her faith. She reflected on her journey thus far, recalling the reasons she embarked on this path in the first place. Fueled by a renewed sense of purpose, she began to seek guidance from mentors and connect with other investors. Learning from their experiences, Maria cultivated the courage to tackle her problems head-on. She started by addressing the repair issues, enlisting help from reputable contractors, and learning the ropes of negotiation to manage costs more effectively.Realizing her original property management approach was flawed, Maria embraced a new perspective. She immersed herself in networking within her community, attending local investor meetups, and engaging with real estate forums online. The connections she made not only provided her with invaluable advice but also opened doors to collaborative opportunities. Maria gradually transformed her failing investment into a learn-and-earn experience. By getting her hands dirty—quite literally—she learned how to manage contractor relationships better, understand her market, and create a workable budget. Importantly, she learned to welcome failure as a teacher rather than a foe.Maria's story is a testament to the idea that resilience is often born from adversity, an idea echoed in the journey of Amir Khan. Amir, a former engineer turned real estate investor, faced his own set of challenges when he ventured into the market. He was initially drawn to real estate due to its potential for passive income, aiming to increase his savings and secure a more comfortable future for his family. His first investment was a small multifamily property, which he purchased with the belief that the rental market in his chosen area would flourish.However, when Amir took possession of the property, he discovered extensive maintenance issues that he had overlooked in his excitement to close the deal. Additionally, the tenant turnover was higher than expected, and within months, he found himself juggling the dual responsibilities of dealing with repairs and looking for new tenants. The moment he realized that his numbers had been overly optimistic, he felt as if the ground had been pulled from under him.The financial pressure was mounting, but Amir knew that giving up was not an option. Instead, he redoubled his efforts, treating his setbacks as an opportunity to sharpen his skills. This journey compelled him to immerse himself in education—he began reading books on property management, attended seminars, and tapped into online resources. Each piece of knowledge became a tool in his belt, helping him approach both his property and his problems from informed angles.One of the most significant lessons Amir learned was about the importance of community. Instead of isolating himself during tough times, he started to engage with local real estate groups. By actively participating in discussions, Amir realized that other investors had faced similar hurdles. These conversations not only provided practical advice on maintaining properties and managing tenants but also fostered a sense of belonging in a field that can often feel isolating.Amir began to implement the practical strategies he had learned, which ultimately transformed his property into a stable source of income. Over time, he was able to build a wealth portfolio and expand into new markets, always carrying those initial lessons forward. Amir's experience highlights an essential truth of resilience: the journey to success is often littered with obstacles, but each setback can lead to a greater understanding and a more profound sense of purpose.Equally inspiring is the journey of Lexi Foster, a real estate investor whose path diverged significantly from her initial plans. Lexi entered the industry with substantial optimism, considering herself a savvy businesswoman ready to capitalize on the real estate boom. She conquered her fear of failure by listening to success stories, believing her investment portfolio would echo those experiences. However, life had other plans.After purchasing her first property, a charming single-family home in a desirable neighborhood, Lexi quickly encountered unexpected challenges. Almost immediately, she was confronted with issues that she had never anticipated—tenants who refused to pay rent, damage from previous tenants that surfaced post-closing, and unexpected municipal regulations that complicated her plans for renovations. Lexi felt trapped, as if all the dreams she had for her new venture were slipping away.In those dark moments, Lexi discovered a reservoir of strength within herself. Rather than succumb to despair, she diligently researched tenant laws and regulations. Armed with critical knowledge, she reached out to legal aid to navigate her tenant problems effectively. At the same time, she adjusted her approach to property renovations, turning them into a phased project that allowed her to manage costs while progressively improving the property.As Lexi became more involved in her community and invested time in fostering relationships with her tenants, she found that open communication became her greatest asset. Building trust and rapport transformed her rental situation, ultimately allowing her to turn her property into not only a profitable investment but a cherished home for her tenants. Lexi's story illustrates that the journey toward success often requires an adaptive mindset and the courage to change course when necessary.The stories of Maria, Amir, and Lexi are just a few among countless narratives of resilience in real estate. They exemplify the power of perseverance and adaptability, qualities that every aspiring investor must cultivate to navigate the inevitable ups and downs of the industry. Each of their journeys underscores a common thread: resilience is not an innate trait but a skill honed through experiences.Building resilience starts with acknowledging the fear of failure. Many investors let the idea of failure paralyze them, holding on to the stigma that failure is synonymous with defeat. However, in embracing the possibility of failure, we create room for growth and learning. Rather than allowing fear to dictate our paths, we must learn to view setbacks as stepping stones toward our goals.Equally crucial is the importance of surrounding oneself with a supportive network. The journeys of Maria, Amir, and Lexi remind us that isolation can worsen setbacks, while connection can breed inspiration and opportunity. An investor's network can offer tremendous insight, and leaning into those relationships can foster resilience. Engaging with mentors, joining community groups, and participating in real estate associations can prove invaluable.In addition, cultivating a mindset of continuous learning is essential. The real estate market is constantly evolving, and investors must remain adaptable to thrive. By seeking knowledge proactively, whether through reading, attending workshops, or engaging with fellow investors, individuals can equip themselves with the tools to better navigate challenges.Moreover, self-reflection plays a significant role in developing resilience. Reflecting on past failures allows investors to uncover hidden lessons, identify patterns in their decision-making, and respond more effectively to future challenges. By analyzing the hurdles faced and the responses yielded, investors can shift their perspectives, focusing on solutions rather than obstacles.Ultimately, resilience in real estate comes down to the willingness to transform failures into opportunities. Each setback, each obstacle, is a chance to learn, grow, and adapt. Investors who embrace the philosophy of resilience will find that, in the face of adversity, they possess the strength to rise again, often stronger and more knowledgeable than before.As we navigate the twists and turns of the real estate journey, let the stories of fellow investors serve as reminders that resilience is a vital ingredient for success. Embrace your setbacks, seek inspiration from others, and nurture your growth; for it is in these experiences that we discover our true potential. The road may be rough, but with resilience as our compass, we can forge ahead, turning failures into stepping stones on our path to fortune.

The Resilience Mindset

The journey of a real estate investor is rarely a straight path. The highs often feel euphoric, lifting spirits to the clouds, while the lows can plummet into despair and self-doubt. In these moments of adversity, the resilience mindset becomes not just beneficial—it becomes a necessity. This subchapter will provide you with actionable steps to cultivate this essential mindset, complete with exercises in visualization, affirmations, and strategies for building a robust support network. Resilience is defined as the ability to bounce back from setbacks. It involves not just surviving difficult situations, but thriving in the face of them. In the world of real estate, where deals can fall through and market conditions can shift unexpectedly, a resilient mindset empowers you to face challenges head-on, turning obstacles into stepping stones. To cultivate this resilience mindset, we begin with an exploration of visualization, a powerful tool that helps you to mentally prepare for both success and adversity. Visualization is the practice of mentally rehearsing your goals and the steps needed to achieve them. Imagine standing at a crossroads in your real estate journey, facing potential pitfalls or challenges. The ability to visualize yourself navigating these difficulties successfully can significantly boost your confidence. 1. **Commit to Regular Visualization Sessions**: Find a quiet space where you can reflect without distractions. Begin by closing your eyes and taking deep, calming breaths. Focus on a specific challenge you are currently facing or one that you anticipate. Picture yourself not only confronting this challenge but navigating it with confidence. Visualize the details—how you feel, the expressions on your face, and even the reactions of those around you. The more vivid your vision, the stronger its impact will be. 2. **Create a Vision Board**: A vision board serves as a tangible representation of your goals and dreams. Gather images, quotes, and phrases that resonate with your aspirations in real estate. Arrange them on a corkboard or poster, creating a collage that inspires you. Place this board in a prominent location, allowing it to serve as a daily reminder of your objectives. As you attract like-minded individuals, consider involving them in the creation of the board. Collective energy can amplify your visualizations. 3. **Set Specific Visual Goals**: Visualize specific outcomes rather than general successes. Instead of merely picturing "being successful," visualize closing a specific deal. Envision every step of the process, from negotiations to final signatures. When you focus on the specifics, your mind begins to strategize real pathways toward those outcomes. Next, we delve into the practice of affirmations. Affirmations are positive statements that can challenge and overcome self-sabotaging thoughts. When repeated often, these positive declarations can help reshape your outlook and enhance your resilience. 1. **Develop a List of Affirmations**: Create personalized affirmations that reflect the resilient mindset you wish to cultivate. For example, you might write, "Every setback is a setup for my comeback," or "I am capable of overcoming any obstacle." Write these affirmations down and repeat them daily, preferably in the morning. Think of them as mental vitamins that nourish your strength and help build your resilience.2. **Turn Negative Thoughts into Affirmations**: Pay attention to your internal dialogue, especially during tough times. When negative thoughts arise, consciously transform them into affirmations. For instance, if you find yourself thinking, "I always fail when I invest," reframe it to, "I learn valuable lessons from every investment I make." This method not only promotes resilience but also fosters an attitude of growth.3. **Affirmations with Visualization**: Combine affirmations with your visualization exercises. As you visualize overcoming challenges, breathe life into those images by saying your affirmations aloud. This dual practice locks in powerful imagery and positive self-talk, encouraging a belief in your ability to bounce back from difficulties.Both visualization and affirmations are potent tools for building a resilient mindset, but they are most effective when combined with a supportive network. Surrounding yourself with like-minded individuals can bolster your emotional growth and provide encouragement during challenging times.1. **Identify Your Tribe**: Building a resilient support network begins with identifying those who share your values. Seek out fellow investors, mentors, or even friends and family who understand the highs and lows of real estate investing. Choose individuals who inspire you and uplift your spirits, rather than those who sap your energy. 2. **Engage in Group Discussions**: Create or join forums, whether online or in person, where you can share experiences, insights, and advice. Engaging in discussions allows you to both give and receive support. When you contribute your own experiences, you reinforce your resilience while inspiring others to navigate their challenges.3. **Mastermind Groups**: Consider forming a mastermind group with fellow real estate investors who are committed to personal and professional growth. These groups offer opportunities for accountability, brainstorming, and collaboration. When you gather with others who share similar ambitions, you create a safe space for sharing setbacks and successes alike, enriching each member's emotional toolkit.4. **Seek Out Mentorship**:

Mentorship can be an invaluable asset. Seek out experienced investors who have faced adversity and emerged stronger. A mentor can provide insights not only on business strategies but also on resilience strategies that proved successful in challenging situations. Their stories can serve as motivation and guidance as you navigate your own path.5. **Celebrate Each Other's Successes**: Resilience is not only about enduring hardship. It's also about celebrating victories, no matter how small. Make it a point to acknowledge and celebrate the successes of your support network. Doing so strengthens relationships and fosters a community where resilience is cultivated and encouraged.6. **Create a "Support Buddy" System**: Pair up with someone in your network to check in regularly. Whether it's a weekly coffee chat or a monthly phone call, having a "support buddy" provides you with a dedicated space to discuss wins, losses, and everything in between. This system can significantly enhance your emotional growth as you share and reflect on your journeys together.In navigating the real estate landscape, you will undoubtedly face setbacks. The importance of maintaining a resilience mindset cannot be overstated. By employing the practices of visualization, affirmations, and fostering a supportive network, you are not merely preparing for the next challenge; you are equipping yourself with a toolkit designed for success.As you embark on these exercises, remember that resilience is not a destination; it's a journey. It requires patience and dedication. Your ability to bounce back will strengthen not only your capacity as an investor but also enrich your personal growth. Embrace each setback as an opportunity for growth, knowing that with the right mindset, you have the power to transform challenges into stepping stones for success.As we continue our exploration of the resilience factor in real estate, keep in mind that cultivating this mindset will yield rewards beyond financial success. It will empower you to lead a life filled with purpose, confidence, and unshakeable faith in your ability to thrive. In every moment of struggle, know that you possess the strength to transform failure into fortune and navigate the trenches of real estate with unwavering resolve.

Chapter 5

CRAFTING A SUCCESS BLUEPRINT

Identifying Goals

In the world of real estate investing, the first step towards success is often a simple but profound one: identifying goals. While it may seem elementary, the act of clearly articulating your aspirations lays the groundwork for everything that follows. "The Visionary Investor," a conceptual archetype we will follow through this subchapter, embodies the journey of setting and revising goals—a process that is essential for any investor at any stage of their career. The Visionary Investor, let's call her Maya, started her real estate journey in her mid-thirties, fueled by a combination of ambition and a desire for financial independence. She had been working a corporate job for over a decade and felt trapped in the 9-to-5 grind. Her dreams of traveling the world, giving her children better educational opportunities, and one day retiring early felt distant. One rainy afternoon, while attending a community seminar on real estate investing, Maya came upon an epiphany: if she wanted to change her life, she had to set clear and achievable goals. Maya's first step was to take a moment and reflect on what she truly desired. She needed more than vague dreams of "financial freedom" or "owning properties." With the guidance of a mentor, she learned to articulate her aspirations in specific, measurable, and time-bound terms. This clarity not only transformed her mindset but also aligned her daily actions with her long-term vision. As she wrote down her goals, she felt a renewed sense of excitement and direction. One of Maya's first goals was to purchase her first rental property within the next year. She envisioned herself walking through the doors of a charming duplex in a neighborhood she had researched. She made a list of what she needed to achieve this: saving a specific amount for a down payment, understanding financing options, and learning how to analyze potential investment properties. By breaking this larger goal into smaller, manageable steps, Maya felt empowered, viewing each milestone not just as a task but as a building block toward her bigger vision. In parallel with specific investments, maximum flexibility was essential. As Maya began to delve deeper into the world of real estate, she recognized that the market is unpredictable. The strategies she envisioned six months prior might need to evolve. With this understanding, she incorporated a practice of regular goal reassessment and revision into her routine. Every quarter, Maya set aside time to review her progress, reflect on challenges, and adjust her goals based on her evolving understanding of the market and her personal circumstances. For instance, six months into her journey, Maya faced an unexpected setback: her bank had changed its lending criteria, making it more challenging for her to secure financing for her first property. Rather than seeing this as failure, she reexamined her financial strategies. During her quarterly review, she not only adjusted her goals but also revisited her action plan. She began to explore alternative financing options, including partnerships and creative financing strategies. This adaptability allowed her to stay focused on her dreams while remaining responsive to market realities. When Maya successfully purchased her first duplex, she celebrated this achievement as a significant milestone that validated her efforts. However, she quickly learned that reaching one goal does not signify the end of the journey. With new experiences and skills under her belt, she outlined her next set of goals: increasing her rental portfolio and eventually moving into property development. The Visionary Investor learned that the journey of real estate investing is cyclical. Each achievement opens doors to new aspirations, and with each transition, the cycle of goal setting and reassessment begins anew. As Maya's portfolio grew, so did her aspirations. Initially focused on single-family homes, her goals shifted toward multi-unit properties, and eventually, she envisioned developing commercial spaces. Herein lies another critical aspect of successful goal setting: the necessity of adaptability and openness to new opportunities. While the foundational goals of securing financial freedom and achieving work-life balance remained, Maya's journey illuminated the importance of allowing her goals to evolve as she gained experience and insight. This transformation was not solely about numbers; it was a holistic endeavor that encompassed her life. Maya included personal goals that expanded beyond financial metrics. She aspired to mentor newcomers in the investing space, commit time to volunteer work, and, most importantly, maintain her family life, which she regarded as foundational to her happiness. As Maya reflected on her progress, she recognized the significant role that faith and resilience played in her journey. There were moments of doubt, times when properties fell through, or when the market downturn seemed insurmountable. Yet, amidst these challenges, she anchored herself in the vision she had created. Each setback transformed into a lesson learned, reinforcing her resolve to keep moving forward. Faith in this context is not merely an abstract notion; it translates into trust—trust in her abilities, in her strategies, and ultimately in the value of actively pursuing her vision. When Maya faced challenges—such as a failed investment opportunity or a market downturn— she chose to learn from those experiences rather than allow them to dictate her future. Her faith was the undercurrent of resilience that propelled her through tough times, reminding her that every setback could serve as a stepping stone to greater success. An essential tool that Maya discovered on her journey was visualization. By regularly visualizing her goals, she created a mental picture that enhanced her motivation and determination. On days when the financial reports were disheartening or when tenant issues arose, she would close her eyes and envision her ultimate success—owner of thriving rental properties, the freedom to travel, the ability to make impactful contributions to her community. This practice served to reaffirm her commitment and courage to continue navigating the ever-changing landscape of real estate. The evolving nature of Maya's goals also opened her eyes to the power of a robust support system. As she became more involved in the real estate community, she formed connections with fellow investors, mentors, and industry experts. Sharing her experiences, successes, and failures fostered an environment of mutual learning and support. This community not only provided emotional encouragement during tough times but also served as a valuable resource for knowledge, advice, and opportunities. Networking became an essential aspect of her growth—attending local real estate meetups, participating in online forums, and joining real estate investment associations. The stories of others who faced similar challenges and overcame them inspired her. The Visionary Investor did not walk alone; each connection added layers to her journey and enriched her understanding of what it meant to invest in real estate. One particularly memorable encounter was with an experienced investor named Thomas, who had been through various market cycles and had witnessed both spectacular successes and notable failures. His candid approach to discussing setbacks resonated with Maya. Thomas emphasized that he viewed each failure not as a roadblock but as a lesson tailored to sharpen his strategies. "Every goal," he said, "should be treated like a negotiation. You have to be prepared to walk away and revisit, but always aim for the deal that serves your vision best." This idea of negotiation extended beyond property deals; it applied to her own aspirations as well. Maya learned to negotiate with her goals: to re-evaluate them when circumstances shifted and to be flexible enough to adapt as her understanding of the market evolved. In doing so, she discovered another layer of resilience that fueled her motivation. Maya's story encapsulates the essence of identifying and articulating goals in real estate investing. Acquiring clarity around her aspirations transformed her approach, allowing her to forge a pathway marked by actionable steps and responsiveness to change. The dual process of setting and revising goals reinforced her faith in the journey and underscored the importance of resilience in the face of setbacks.For readers who find themselves at various points along their own investing journeys, the core takeaway is to embrace the adaptability of goal setting. Whether you are just starting or have been investing for years, remember that clarity in vision, coupled with resilience in execution, will pave the way toward success. Your goals are not static; they should evolve as your experiences broaden and as you gain deeper insights into the transactional world of real estate.As you embark on your own path as an investor, consider the lessons from Maya's journey. Write down your aspirations, break them into actionable steps, and schedule regular assessments of your progress. Embrace flexibility, and don't hesitate to revise your goals in light of new information or experiences. Surround yourself with a supportive network, and, above all, maintain faith in your ability to navigate the complexities of real estate investing.In conclusion, the endeavor of setting and identifying goals is far more than a means to an end; it is a significant part of the journey itself. The Visionary Investor illustrates that every real estate investment story begins with a well-articulated vision, which requires commitment, adaptability, and an unwavering belief in the possibilities that lie ahead. Your vision is your compass; allow it to guide you as you navigate the trenches of real estate investing, turning failures into stepping stones toward lasting success.

Creating a Plan of Action

Creating a Plan of ActionThe journey of a real estate investor is often fraught with challenges, disappointments, and setbacks. However, those who succeed do not simply rely on chance or hope to put them on the path to victory. Instead, they meticulously create plans of action that turn their dreams into attainable goals. In this subchapter, we will delve deeply into how to craft a robust plan of action, transforming the abstract idea of "success" into a structured, step-by-step process that effectively leads to real results. We will begin by establishing the importance of understanding your objectives. Only when you have a clear vision of what you want to achieve can you start laying down the groundwork for your action plan. Many aspiring investors struggle with the vastness of the real estate landscape, feeling overwhelmed by the multitude of possible avenues to explore. The first step in countering this feeling is defining your objectives. Objectives should be SMART: specific, measurable, attainable, relevant, and time-bound. A great way to get started is by writing down your long-term goals. What does success look like for you? Maybe you envision owning multiple properties, building a portfolio that generates passive income, or perhaps you're focused on flipping houses for profit. Write down your most ambitious objectives, no matter how grand they may seem. Just remember, each goal must be broken down into smaller, actionable steps. Next, let's shift our focus to breaking down those overarching goals into manageable, bite-sized chunks. This step is crucial; the tendency to look at the mountain in front of you rather than focusing on putting one foot in front of the other is common and can be paralyzing. Begin by identifying key milestones that will lead you toward your goal. For example, if your objective is to buy your first rental property within the next year, you can break it down as follows:1. **Research the Market (Month 1)**: Spend the first month familiarizing yourself with neighborhoods, property types, and market trends. This knowledge will serve as the foundation for your subsequent decisions.2. **Determine Your Budget (Month 1)**: Identify how much you can invest. This includes calculating not just the purchase price, but also closing costs, renovation expenses, and ongoing operational costs.3. **Build Your Network (Month 2)**: Start connecting with real estate agents, fellow investors, mortgage brokers, etc. Networking is essential in real estate, as a solid contact base can provide you valuable insights, opportunities, and support.4. **Get Pre-Approved for Financing (Month 3)**: Before you can make an offer on a property, you need to know how much you can borrow. Gather your financial documents and approach lenders to figure out your financing options.5. **Begin Property Hunting (Months 4-6)**: Armed with your knowledge and financial backing, start looking for properties that meet your criteria. This process might require visiting multiple listings, attending open houses, and leveraging your network.6. **Make an Offer (Month 6)**: Once you've found a property you're interested in, it's time to make an offer. Ensure you have done your due diligence, including comparative market analysis and property inspections.7. **Negotiate and Close (Month 7)**: Be prepared to negotiate terms. Once your offer is accepted, you'll proceed to finalize financing and complete the closing process.Using a timeline helps create a sense of urgency while making the journey more manageable. Ensure that these chunks are realistic; unrealistic expectations can lead to frustration and ultimately derail your progress. Regularly revisit and adjust your plan to stay aligned with your goals.Developing a plan of action also involves identifying potential obstacles you might face along the way. Anticipating setbacks and challenges enables you to devise contingency plans. For instance, if you find a property you love but might struggle with financing, consider having alternate financial options in place, whether through partnerships, investors, or alternative lending avenues. Moreover, setting up a system to track your progress is invaluable. Create a journal or digital document to record your achievements, milestones, and lessons learned. Celebrating small victories is crucial for morale, especially during challenging periods when your resilience might be tested. Keep abreast of changing market conditions, and adjust your strategies as needed, but never lose sight of your ultimate objective. In addition to setting timelines and tracking progress, developing a habit of constant learning is imperative. Stay informed about market trends, new technologies, and evolving investment strategies. This commitment to continuous improvement will empower you to adapt your plans as circumstances change, ensuring that you remain ahead of the curve. Another essential component of creating an effective action plan is accountability. Consider finding a mentor or joining an investment group. Surrounding yourself with like-minded individuals can serve as motivation and provide a wealth of insights. Sharing your goals with others and regularly discussing your progress will help you remain committed to your plan. Furthermore, it's crucial to have faith in the process and in yourself. Building a successful real estate portfolio is not a sprint; it's a marathon. The road may not always be smooth, but having faith during the tougher times will keep your spirit alive and your focus sharp. Recognize that setbacks can provide the best teaching moments—they are not the end of your journey, but rather a part of it.Additionally, as you build your plan, acknowledge the importance of your mindset. Cultivating a positive attitude can significantly impact your results. When faced with challenges, remind yourself of your "why"—the reasons you set out on this journey. Your drive and passion can serve as a strong motivator, especially when the path becomes steep.No action plan is static. As you progress, regularly revisit and refine your goals based on new insights and experiences. Market conditions may shift, personal circumstances may shift, and once-unforeseen opportunities may present themselves. Embrace flexibility in your plan, as rigidity can lead to missed chances.Now that we've outlined the essential elements of a successful plan of action, let's explore some practical tools and resources you can employ to ensure the efficiency and efficacy of your strategy. Consider utilizing various project management apps available to help you keep track of your tasks, deadlines, and milestones. Tools like Trello or Asana can provide visual representations of your journey, helping you maintain focus.Networking is crucial, but so is learning. Consider online courses or workshops focused on real estate investing strategies. Websites like Coursera or even local community colleges may offer classes that enhance your knowledge base. Additionally, establish a reading list of influential books and articles in the industry, as they can provide valuable perspectives and reinforce your learning. You might also find it beneficial to leverage the power of digital platforms for marketing purposes. Whether you plan to utilize social media to showcase your properties or to tap into real estate listing sites, having a digital presence can expand your reach and connect you with potential buyers or partners. As you embark on this journey, keep in mind that the art of real estate investing does not solely rely on the numbers; it's also about relationships. Building genuine and reciprocal connections with clients, lenders, agents, and even competitors can open doors you never knew existed. Stay open, stay engaged, and never underestimate the power of community. Throughout this subchapter, we have highlighted the importance of creating a plan of action, breaking down your goals, anticipating challenges, and remaining adaptable. Your ability to transform failures into lessons depends largely on how well-prepared you are to navigate the twists and turns that come your way. In conclusion, as you draft your action plan, remember that the content of these plans alone is not sufficient. The real key lies in the commitment to execute them, the perseverance to stay the course amid adversity, and the faith to believe that every failure can ultimately lead to success. Embrace the challenges, learn from your experiences, and let your plan be your trusted guide in the world of real estate investing. Your journey has just begun, and victory awaits those who prepare and dare to take action.

Adapting the Blueprint Over Time

As markets evolve, so too should strategies. The world of real estate is not static; it is a dynamic landscape shaped by economic shifts, demographic changes, technological advancements, and societal trends. For aspiring investors, the ability to adapt is not just a strategy—it is a prerequisite for survival and success. In this subchapter, we will explore the importance of regular assessments and necessary adjustments in crafting a success blueprint. Using real-world examples of successful investors who have demonstrated the power of pivoting to stay relevant, we will highlight the need for flexibility and the commitment required to turn challenges into opportunities.When embarking on a real estate investment journey, it is all too easy to become attached to a particular strategy or methodology. After all, the comfort of familiarity can be enticing. However, sticking rigidly to an outdated plan can lead to complacency and stagnation. Markets are influenced by a multitude of factors that can change at a moment's notice. Interest rates can rise or fall, new regulations can emerge, buyer preferences can shift, and global events can cause local markets to react unpredictably. Those who cannot adapt find themselves at a distinct disadvantage, while those who embrace change position themselves for continued success.Take, for instance, the story of Sarah Jennings, an investor who began her journey in the multi-family residential sector. In the early 2010s, Sarah saw considerable success by acquiring small apartment buildings in a bustling metropolitan area. Her approach was methodical: she would identify underappreciated properties, focus on key renovations to increase their value, and then either hold or sell for profit. However, as the market heated up, the competition became fierce, and the acquisition of these properties became significantly more challenging. Rather than doubling down on her original strategy and succumbing to frustration, Sarah decided to assess the situation. She connected with various industry experts, attended real estate seminars, and conducted thorough market research. What she discovered was a shift in demand from traditional rental models to short-term rentals. With tourism on the rise and local regulations favoring short-stay accommodations, Sarah pivoted her strategy accordingly. She began acquiring properties with the sole intention of converting them into Airbnb rentals, a move that allowed her to capitalize on the booming vacation rental market.Sarah's story exemplifies the first crucial lesson in adapting your blueprint: recognize the signs of change in your market. Regular assessments are key to understanding when it's time to pivot. This means actively seeking out information, listening to market trends, and being open to feedback. It can be helpful to set a schedule for these assessments; whether quarterly or biannually, ensure that you are evaluating your portfolio and strategy regularly. The process of assessment involves both qualitative and quantitative analysis. Looking at data such as occupancy rates, rental prices, and demographic shifts will provide insights into market trends. Equally important is the qualitative aspect—understanding the sentiment of the market. Conversations with other investors, watching what industry leaders are promoting, and even surveying potential tenants can yield invaluable information. Adaptation is not just about a knee-jerk reaction to immediate market conditions, however. It's also about foresight. Investors who succeed in the long run tend to have a keen ability to predict where the market is headed. For example, consider the case of Tom Richards, a commercial real estate investor. Tom began investing in office spaces in urban areas during a period of growth for remote work. Although many in the industry believed that office spaces would always be in demand, Tom's intuition and market perception suggested otherwise. To ensure that he remained ahead of the curve, Tom began to analyze trends in workforce dynamics, studying how companies were reshaping their office needs in response to an increasingly remote workforce. Instead of investing in new office construction, Tom shifted his approach to adaptive reuse projects, turning outdated office complexes into mixed-use spaces that blended office, retail, and residential units. This not only addressed the immediate needs of the market but also catered to a long-term shift in lifestyle and work arrangements. Tom's ability to analyze emerging trends and adapt his investment philosophy accordingly demonstrates a crucial element of adapting the blueprint: foresight. As you navigate the complexities of real estate, it's important to remain curious and observant. Attend industry conferences, keep up with economic reports, and connect with thought leaders in the field. This ongoing education will arm you with the necessary insights to anticipate changes and act proactively rather than reactively. Another aspect of adaptation involves harnessing the power of technology. The real estate industry has seen a tremendous transformation driven by technological advancements. From virtual reality home tours to machine learning algorithms predicting market shifts, technology has created both opportunities and challenges. The investors who thrive are those who understand and integrate technology into their strategies. Take the example of Linda Zhang, a young investor who started her career by focusing on fix-and-flip projects. For years, she relied on traditional methods of analyzing properties based purely on location and comparable sales. However, when she discovered data analytics tools and platforms that could predict home value trends, Linda immediately recognized their potential. She began utilizing sophisticated software that analyzed market conditions, neighborhood statistics, and buyer behavior, allowing her to identify properties that were not only undervalued but also had the highest potential for profit.Linda's decision to embrace technology illustrates how staying current with tools and resources is essential for adaptability. In a world where data is king, leveraging analytics can provide competitive advantages that become increasingly vital in saturated markets. Moreover, utilizing technology for project management, tenant communication, and marketing efforts can enhance operational efficiencies and lead to better bottom-line results.While adaptability is crucial, it's equally important to remain anchored in your overarching vision and values. As you make adjustments to your strategy, ensure that the core of your investment approach aligns with your long-term goals. Flexibility does not mean sacrificing your principles or quality, but rather refining how you achieve your objectives based on changing circumstances. A powerful illustration of this balance can be seen in the journey of Michael Stevens, who established a successful real estate firm focused on sustainable development. As the conversations around sustainability gained traction, Michael realized that while there was a growing demand for eco-friendly living spaces, his firm needed to adjust its approach to keep pace with the changing market. Instead of abandoning his core mission—developing properties that prioritize environmental responsibility—Michael pivoted by innovating how he presented his projects. He began to incorporate cutting-edge green technologies, enhancing the energy efficiency of his buildings and utilizing sustainable materials. Furthermore, he aligned his marketing strategy to highlight the benefits of sustainable living, reaching an audience increasingly concerned with climate impact. This dual focus on adaptation and alignment of values resulted in renewed interest from investors and tenants alike, expanding his business in ways that transcended his initial blueprint.As you evaluate your success blueprint, consider how you can maintain your mission and values while still allowing room for evolution. Embrace a mindset of continuous learning and improvement, recognizing that change is an inherent part of growth. The most successful investors understand that their strategies must evolve, but their fundamental commitment to their vision remains unwavering.Moreover, the importance of networking and building relationships cannot be overlooked when adapting your blueprint. The real estate world is filled with experienced individuals and industry leaders who have weathered market fluctuations. Their insights can provide guidance when it comes to assessing the landscape and adjusting your strategies. Take, for example, the story of Karen Patel, who embodies the essence of collaboration in her investment journey. In her early years, Karen operated primarily in isolation, relying solely on her instincts to guide her decisions. However, as she expanded her portfolio, she realized the value of forming connections with other investors, mentors, and industry experts. Karen began attending local real estate meetups, joining professional networks, and engaging with online communities. What she discovered was a treasure trove of knowledge and experiences that others were willing to share. When the market began to shift, she found herself equipped with fresh perspectives and innovative ideas from her peers, inspiring her to evaluate her portfolio in a new light. As she developed relationships with others in her field, she not only gained allies but also broadened her scope of understanding about market fluctuations.Networking also fosters collaboration and can lead to partnerships that enhance your adaptability. Consider forming joint ventures with other investors to share resources, knowledge, and risks when exploring new markets or strategies. Collaborative efforts can lead to creative solutions that might not have been possible in isolation.Ultimately, the journey of adapting your blueprint is about cultivating resilience. The road to success in real estate is rarely linear; it is filled with hurdles, lessons, and occasional setbacks. Rather than viewing challenges as insurmountable obstacles, view them as opportunities for growth and development. Your ability to adapt is a testament to your resilience, allowing you to bounce back stronger and more informed after each setback.As you move forward in your real estate investing journey, keep a few principles in mind. First and foremost, develop a mindset of curiosity and openness. Embrace the belief that learning should never cease. Your willingness to ask questions, seek knowledge, and explore new avenues will be your greatest asset. Regularly assess your strategies, seek out market trends, and analyze data to stay ahead.Secondly, cultivate relationships and engage with your peers. The insights you gain from networking can serve as the foundation for your adaptability, providing you with diverse perspectives that will enhance your decision-making. Collaboration is not just a strategy; it is a mindset that fosters growth and innovation.Lastly, remember that sticking to your core values is paramount. Adaptation does not mean compromising the principles that define you as an investor. Instead, navigate the changing tides while remaining rooted in your commitment to your vision. Resilience is about bending without breaking, allowing yourself to transform and flourish, even in the face of adversity.In conclusion, adapting your success blueprint is a dynamic process that requires ongoing evaluation, foresight, and a willingness to embrace change. By learning from successful investors who have pivoted seamlessly to remain relevant, you can equip yourself with the tools to navigate the ever-changing world of real estate. Remain flexible, stay informed, and ensure that your decisions align with your core values. Trust in your ability to adapt, and step boldly into the future of your real estate investing journey.

Chapter 6

NETWORKING: BUILDING BRIDGES

The Power of Connections

In the world of real estate, the adage "It's not what you know, but who you know" rings particularly true. While knowledge, skills, and market analysis are vital components of success in this industry, the power of connections cannot be underestimated. Networking serves as the lifeblood of real estate investment. It is a dynamic process that fosters professional relationships, nurtures strategic partnerships, and ultimately paves the way for significant business opportunities. In this subchapter, we will delve into the profound impact of networking, illustrating how relationships can drive growth and development in real estate. At its core, networking is about building bridges. These connections transcend transactional interactions, creating robust relationships that often manifest into collaborative ventures. In real estate, the players extend far beyond buyers and sellers. There are agents, brokers, lenders, investors, contractors, lawyers, and countless other professionals involved in the process. Each of these individuals possesses unique insights and expertise that can significantly influence an investor's journey. The ability to forge and maintain these connections can serve as a catalyst for success, particularly during challenging times.To understand the significance of networking, we must consider the stories of those who have thrived in the real estate sector. One such narrative is that of Sarah, a novice investor who broke into the market during the Great Recession. When she first entered the field, Sarah was overwhelmed by the breadth of knowledge required to navigate real estate. With very little capital and a shaky understanding of financing, she felt like she was swimming against the tide. However, Sarah soon realized that she needed to leverage the potential of networking to propel her forward.She began attending local real estate investment group meetings, where she encountered individuals who would ultimately become her mentors. Through these connections, Sarah learned about key financing avenues she had never considered. One of her newfound acquaintances, a seasoned investor named Mark, shared his experience in negotiating private loans. His guidance opened doors to funding opportunities that were previously inaccessible to her. Sarah's story exemplifies how relationships can transform an investor's landscape, turning barriers into pathways of progress.As entrepreneurs, real estate investors often find themselves in the midst of uncertainty. The changing market conditions, fluctuating interest rates, and evolving regulations can all create a sense of instability. In such environments, the value of a solid network becomes even more pronounced. When challenges arise, having a network of trusted allies can provide not just advice and insights but also emotional support. Networking becomes a form of resilience, allowing investors to weather storms and collaborate on solutions.Take the experience of Daniel, another investor who faced significant setbacks early in his career. Daniel had invested in a series of properties that ultimately fell short of generating the desired returns. During this difficult period, he reached out to his network for support. He connected with fellow investors who had faced similar challenges. Sharing strategies, resources, and experiences, this group offered both practical guidance and encouragement. Through these collaborative efforts, Daniel not only salvaged his investments but also transformed his approach to real estate.

The relationships he cultivated during this phase proved invaluable as he emerged stronger and more informed.Collaboration is often the bedrock of successful real estate deals. Through concerted efforts, investors can pool their resources, share risks, and amplify their purchasing power. Joint ventures have become a popular approach to navigating the complexities of the market. For example, when Quinton sought to invest in a large multifamily project, he knew he would require more capital than what he could provide alone. Instead of pursuing an isolated route, he reached out to several connections on his network. By forming a joint venture with two partners, Quinton not only secured the necessary funding but also benefited from diverse perspectives that enriched the project. Their collaboration ultimately led to a successful acquisition and profitable investment.The importance of networking extends beyond securing funds and finding business partners. Relationships can also play a pivotal role in vendor selection, which can influence the profitability and sustainability of real estate investments. A reliable contractor or a skilled property manager can make all the difference in an investor's experience. Networking allows investors to tap into recommendations and referrals that can guide them toward trustworthy professionals. Consider Mia, who was navigating her first large renovation project. Unsure of where to turn for reliable contractors, she leaned on her network. Through discussions with fellow investors, she received several recommendations, each paired with personal anecdotes about the quality of work and reliability. By tapping into the wisdom of her connections, Mia was able to assemble a team that exceeded her expectations and kept her project on time and on budget. The landscape of the real estate industry continues to evolve, driven by technological advancements and changing consumer behaviors. As these shifts occur, maintaining connections becomes critical to staying ahead of the curve. Networking offers investors access to industry trends and emerging opportunities that may not yet be widely publicized. Engaging with industry experts, attending seminars, and participating in webinars can provide insights into the latest market developments. Jasmine, a driven real estate entrepreneur, recognized the power of innovation in her field. By attending various industry conferences and expos, she surrounded herself with thought leaders who were shaping the future of real estate. Conversations led to invaluable discussions about new real estate technologies, opportunities in sustainable housing, and innovative financing solutions. The networks she cultivated during these events not only expanded her knowledge but also resulted in partnerships that would strengthen her business in the long term.Establishing a solid network requires intentionality and effort. Aspiring investors need to cultivate these relationships actively rather than leaving them to chance. The first step is to engage with local investment groups, chambers of commerce, and real estate associations. Online platforms, such as LinkedIn, also provide opportunities to connect with industry professionals and expand networks beyond geographic boundaries.Equally important, however, is the need to create value within these relationships. Networking is not merely about what one can gain but also how one can contribute. Building a reputation as a reliable resource amplifies the impact of connection. By sharing insights, offering support, and being willing to help others in their journeys, investors cultivate a sense of community. Consider the case of Jose, who began his networking journey by volunteering at a local real estate charity event. Not only did this experience allow him to meet seasoned investors and industry professionals, but it also ingrained in him the importance of giving back. By actively contributing to others' success, he laid the groundwork for lasting relationships. Over time, these connections have led to numerous collaborative opportunities, partnerships, and recommendations that continue to benefit his burgeoning real estate career.As the adage goes, "The more you give, the more you receive." In the world of networking, this principle holds true. Building strong relationships requires time, trust, and reciprocal value. While nurturing connections, it is essential to maintain authenticity and sincerity. The genuine pursuit of mutually beneficial partnerships fosters long-lasting relationships that can withstand industry fluctuations.Networking is not without its challenges. Building and maintaining these connections can be time-consuming, which can overwhelm newcomers focusing on deal-making. Additionally, the fear of rejection can deter individuals from reaching out to potential connections. However, embracing vulnerability and taking proactive steps toward initiating relationships can lead to profound transformations in an investor's journey.Overcoming these barriers often begins with shifting one's mindset. Viewing networking as an opportunity rather than a daunting task creates a positive context for engagement. Approach connections with curiosity and openness, seeking to learn from others' experiences and share one's own insights. When conversations flow from a place of genuine interest, relationships naturally flourish.As we reflect on the stories shared throughout this subchapter, it becomes clear that networking is not merely an auxiliary skill in real estate; it is an essential cornerstone of success. The triumphs of Sarah, Daniel, Quinton, Mia, Jasmine, and Jose illustrate that building bridges through relationships creates pathways to new opportunities. Collaboration overshadows competition, and together, investors can navigate the complexities with greater resilience and creativity.Ultimately, the power of connections lies in their ability to transform challenges into stepping stones toward success. Navigating the trenches of real estate investment necessitates not just knowledge and skill but also a community of like-minded individuals willing to share, support, and innovate together. As aspiring investors step into this vibrant arena, may they remember that the key to unlocking the doors of opportunity often rests in the strength of their connections. Embrace the journey of networking, for it is the relationship-building endeavors that will turn setbacks into triumphs and dreams into reality.

Building Meaningful Relationships

In the world of real estate investing, networking is not just a professional necessity; it is a powerful tool that can shape your trajectory in the industry. The relationships you build can serve as a foundation for shared knowledge, support during challenging times, and opportunities that may not be accessible otherwise. In this subchapter, we will explore practical strategies to effectively network within the real estate arena, emphasizing the importance of active listening, authenticity, and the emotional nuances that come with building meaningful relationships.As an aspiring real estate investor, it is imperative to approach networking with the mindset that the relationships you cultivate are more than just transactions; they are connections with potential mentors, partners, and friends. It is easy to get caught up in the hustle of making connections for personal gain. However, the most successful investors understand that real, lasting relationships are mutual; they require authenticity, sincerity, and, most importantly, a genuine interest in the people you meet.Imagine attending an industry conference filled with potential partners, investors, and thought leaders. The atmosphere buzzes with conversations, the exchange of ideas, and the excitement of collaboration. As you step into this whirlwind, how do you ensure that your presence counts? The key lies in being fully present, actively listening, and engaging meaningfully.Active listening is not merely about hearing what others say; it is about understanding and absorbing the information they share. This practice creates a deeper level of connection and signals to others that you value their experiences and insights. When engaging in discussions, pause before responding. Reflect on their words. Ask thoughtful follow-up questions that encourage them to elaborate on their experiences or insights. For instance, suppose you meet a seasoned investor at a networking event who shares their journey of overcoming challenges in a highly competitive market. Instead of launching into your own story or pitching your latest project, consider delving deeper into their experience. Ask questions like, "What motivated you to continue investing despite those setbacks?" or "How did you pivot your strategy during that challenging time?" These inquiries not only foster a more meaningful conversation but also demonstrate your interest in learning from their journey and insights.Authenticity is another cornerstone of meaningful connections. In a highly competitive environment like real estate, it's easy to feel compelled to showcase only your successes. However, embracing vulnerability and sharing your struggles can foster genuine connections. When you're open about your journey—both the triumphs and failures—you invite others to do the same. This act of sharing builds trust and allows you to form deeper bonds that go beyond superficial networking.Consider the story of a young investor who found herself struggling during her first property flip. At a local real estate meetup, she was reluctant to share her challenges, fearing judgment from more experienced investors. However, when she finally opened up about her fears and the difficulties she faced, she was surprised to find that many in the room had faced similar hurdles. In that safe space, several attendees offered advice and encouragement, fostering a sense of community. By embracing her authenticity, she attracted individuals who genuinely wanted to support her journey, transforming the network into a tight-knit community that provided ongoing guidance and friendship.As you navigate networking opportunities, remember to be intentional about the relationships you pursue. It's not about the quantity of connections but the quality that determines the depth of your network. Before attending an event, take some time to research who will be there, and identify a few individuals you genuinely want to connect with. Prepare thoughtful questions tailored to their experiences in the industry, allowing for discussions that highlight your interest in their expertise.In addition to industry events, online platforms present a valuable avenue for networking in today's digital age. Social media platforms such as LinkedIn, for instance, provide a unique opportunity to connect with a wide array of professionals. However, it's important to remember that online interactions can often feel impersonal. Therefore, approach your online networking with the same authenticity and active listening that you would in person. When connecting with someone online, take the time to personalize your outreach. Reference a post they shared or a mutual connection, and express genuine interest in their work. For example, if you come across a LinkedIn article written by an investor you admire, don't hesitate to comment thoughtfully on the piece before reaching out. This demonstrates not only your engagement but also your commitment to building a connection grounded in shared interests and mutual respect. In the spirit of fostering authentic connections, consider participating in online communities and forums dedicated to real estate investing. Platforms like BiggerPockets offer a vibrant community for investors to share experiences, ask questions, and provide advice. Within these digital spaces, practice active listening by engaging in discussions, offering insights from your journey, and respecting diverse opinions. Over time, you may find yourself forming connections that extend beyond the online realm. Local meetups still hold an irreplaceable spot in the networking ecosystem. These gatherings create an intimate setting for aspiring investors and seasoned veterans to share experiences over refreshments. Attending meetups can be an invaluable source of inspiration, education, and relationship-building. However, to navigate these gatherings effectively, approach them with clear intentions. Before attending a meetup, take a moment to set goals. Are you looking for a mentor, a fellow investor to collaborate with on a project, or simply to learn from others' experiences? Having a target in mind can help you navigate the event more purposefully. When you arrive, engage in conversations with a sense of openness. Ask for business cards and offer your own, ensuring that you follow up with a personal message post-event to reinforce the connection. Throughout this networking journey, it is essential to maintain a balance between giving and receiving. Be generous with your time and resources; offer assistance to others when you can. When you genuinely seek to help others achieve their goals, you create a positive ripple effect that often returns to you in unexpected ways. Build your reputation as someone who is approachable, willing to share knowledge, and ready to lend a hand. This attitude not only enriches your connections but positions you as a valuable member of the community.As you cultivate relationships, remember that the path of real estate investing is often fraught with challenges. It is during these trying times that the strength of your network truly reveals itself. When you encounter a setback, having trusted individuals to lean on can make all the difference. Keep communication lines open with your network and don't hesitate to reach out when you need advice, support, or a listening ear.Take the example of an investor who faced a sudden economic downturn, impacting multiple projects at once. Instead of retreating into isolation, he leveraged his network for support. He sought advice from seasoned mentors, collaborated with colleagues facing similar challenges, and even participated in group brainstorming sessions. This collaborative approach not only alleviated his burden but also fostered a sense of shared resilience within the community.In nurturing relationships, always be mindful of reciprocity. Relationships should never feel one-sided; they thrive on the mutual exchange of support, knowledge, and opportunities. As you share your own experiences and insights, be open to receiving guidance from others. This dynamic creates a sense of community and establishes a network that can weather both personal and industry storms.Throughout this process, be patient with yourself. Building meaningful relationships takes time and consistency. Rather than seeking instant gratification or immediate results, focus on the long-term value of each connection you make. Approach networking as a journey that enriches your experience within the real estate industry, allowing you to learn and grow alongside your peers.Reflecting on the emotional side of networking, remember that relationships often hinge on shared values, experiences, and aspirations. The most impactful connections are forged through vulnerability, trust, and a commitment to mutual growth. Embrace the journey of connecting with others, allowing yourself to be both a mentor and a mentee. As you develop your network, you'll find yourself surrounded by individuals who inspire you, challenge you, and propel you toward success.In conclusion, building meaningful relationships within the real estate community is a vital aspect of navigating challenges and achieving success. By practicing active listening, embracing authenticity, and fostering a spirit of giving, you can create a network that supports your goals and enriches your journey. Remember that these connections are not just transactional; they can become a source of encouragement and inspiration that transforms failures into stepping stones toward your greater aspirations. The relationships you build today will lay the groundwork for the successes of tomorrow. Approach networking not just as an obligation, but as an opportunity to cultivate partnerships and friendships that will resonate throughout your career.

Leveraging Network Dynamics

In the realm of real estate investment, the power of networking cannot be overstated. It serves as a lifeline, connecting individuals to opportunities, resources, and support. This subchapter, "Leveraging Network Dynamics," delves into the mechanics of building a robust network that can propel your career forward, particularly in the challenging landscape of real estate. It is through the relationships we cultivate that we can turn setbacks into successes, and understanding how to leverage these network dynamics can be a game changer for aspiring investors.The importance of a supportive network cannot be underestimated. In business, like in life, we do not succeed in isolation. We often rely on the expertise, insights, and encouragement of others. This is especially true in the competitive field of real estate, where challenges are numerous and the path to success is often fraught with obstacles. To navigate these complexities effectively, aspiring investors must engage actively with their networks, reinforcing relationships that can provide guidance and open doors to untapped potential.A critical aspect of leveraging network dynamics is the identification of mentorship opportunities. The figure of the mentor is vital in any professional sector, and real estate is no exception. Mentors offer a wealth of experience and knowledge that can help you sidestep common pitfalls and build a solid foundation for your investment journey. A mentor offers a unique perspective, having navigated the same landscape you aspire to conquer. In this journey, one influential character emerges: The Mentor Sage. The Mentor Sage embodies the wisdom and experience gained over years of navigating the real estate market. Imagine a seasoned investor, perhaps in their late fifties or sixties, whose own journey has been marked by both triumphs and setbacks. This mentor not only possesses a vast understanding of the industry but also a desire to give back to the next generation of investors. The Mentor Sage serves as a guiding light for aspiring investors, paving their way through networks that have been carefully curated over the years.Engaging with a mentor requires humility and openness. It necessitates the willingness to learn, to ask questions, and to accept constructive criticism. Meetings with The Mentor Sage might take place in an informal setting over coffee or in more structured environments like workshops and seminars. Each interaction becomes an opportunity for growth.During one of these meetings, a budding investor named Alex takes the initiative to ask The Mentor Sage about navigating the ups and downs of real estate markets. "How do you stay focused when uncertain conditions arise?" Alex inquires, reflecting a common concern among new investors who may feel overwhelmed by market volatility. The Mentor Sage smiles knowingly, leaning back in their chair. "The truth is, uncertainty is part of real estate. Markets go up and down, but your focus should remain on your long-term goals. Build a resilient mindset. Surround yourself with a supportive network of professionals who can offer sound advice during downturns. That connection could mean the difference between stagnation and growth."This exchange encapsulates the essence of mentorship: gaining insights that allow you to view your challenges through a new lens. By adopting the perspective of the Mentor Sage, aspiring investors learn to navigate uncertainties with confidence, preparing them for the relentless fluctuations that the real estate market can present.In addition to securing a mentor, aspiring investors should actively seek peer groups that foster collaboration and mutual support. These groups can manifest in various forms, such as local real estate investment associations, online forums, or mastermind groups. Engaging with peers allows investors to share experiences, strategies, and lessons learned, forming a collective strength that amplifies individual efforts.Consider the interactions within one such peer group. Members gather regularly to discuss their latest ventures, challenges, and aspirations. Each meeting is a melting pot of ideas where aspiring investors can present their latest projects and seek feedback. This environment not only nurtures professional growth but also cultivates camaraderie, making the journey more enjoyable and less daunting.In one of these gatherings, a member named Jamie presents a recent deal that fell through, detailing the stakes, the emotions involved, and the aftermath of the experience. "I feel like I've let my investors down," Jamie admits, frustration etched on their face. The room falls silent for a moment, and then The Mentor Sage, who has been observing quietly from the corner, leans in."First of all, you didn't fail; you learned. Every setback is a stepping stone toward your success. Use this experience to refine your approach. As for your investors, communicate transparently. They'll appreciate your honesty, and this will strengthen the relationship," the mentor gently counsels.Herein lies another valuable lesson gleaned from network dynamics: failure shared is failure lessened. By bringing vulnerabilities to the group and allowing others to share in those moments, investors realize they are not alone in their struggles. The peer group acts as a sounding board, providing a safety net where individuals can take risks without the fear of isolation.Collaboration strategies are also an integral part of leveraging your network. Forming partnerships with other investors, agents, contractors, and other professionals can lead to mutually beneficial outcomes. A synergetic approach allows all parties involved to pool resources, share risks, and create greater opportunities for success.For instance, two investors, Priya and Mark, decide to collaborate on a project that requires expertise in different areas. Priya excels in property management while Mark has a knack for identifying promising investment opportunities. By combining their strengths, they mitigate the risks associated with a project that each would find overwhelming on their own. Meetings occur regularly to discuss project updates, address concerns, and strategize future steps. When entering a collaboration, it is crucial to clarify expectations and establish a joint vision. Effective communication serves as the bedrock for successful collaborations, ensuring all parties are aligned with the project's goals and objectives. The Mentor Sage often advises that partners need to remain adaptable, willing to adjust course when challenges arise. "What if things start to go off the rails?" one group member asks during a brainstorming session. The Mentor Sage, ever prepared to share their wisdom, responds, "Flexibility is key. Allow for adjustments while keeping the bigger picture in focus. Communicate openly, and never forget why you decided to collaborate in the first place." This approach ensures that relationships remain intact even when faced with hurdles. It cultivates a sense of loyalty and respect, allowing investors to navigate both the highs and lows of their ventures together. Networking dynamics extend beyond mere connections; they involve nurturing and maintaining these relationships over time. Regular check-ins with mentors, peers, and collaborators are essential for keeping those connections vibrant. This could involve sharing industry insights, celebrating milestones, or offering support during tough times. Such acts of engagement not only deepen relationships but also create a reciprocal environment where collaboration flourishes. One effective way to maintain these relationships is through continued education. The real estate landscape is ever-evolving, with new regulations, technologies, and market trends emerging regularly. By attending workshops, webinars, and conferences, aspiring investors can connect with their network while simultaneously enhancing their knowledge base. This dual approach reinforces their commitment to personal and professional growth. The Mentor Sage insists upon the importance of lifelong learning, often sharing their own experiences of adapting to changes in the market. "I can't stress enough how staying informed has set me apart from others in the industry. When you invest in your education, you're indirectly investing in your network. You become a resource who others will look to for guidance," they explain.Ultimately, leveraging network dynamics to foster growth and support relies heavily on reciprocity. As you engage with mentors, peers, and collaborators, remember that building bridges is a two-way street. Offer your expertise, support others in their ventures, and contribute to the conversations. Your willingness to invest in others can yield rich rewards, creating a culture of assistance where everyone involved can thrive. In conclusion, navigating the challenges of real estate investment requires more than just market knowledge and a keen sense for opportunity. By understanding how to leverage network dynamics, aspiring investors can unlock an expansive realm of growth and support. Through mentorship, peer collaborations, and nurturing relationships, they can turn setbacks into learning experiences and ultimately lead themselves toward sustained success. Faith in these connections empowers investors to remain resilient in the face of adversity, transforming every challenge into a stepping stone on their journey toward accomplishment. Embrace the strength found within your network and let it guide you as you forge your path in the intricate world of real estate.

Chapter 7

LEARNING TO PIVOT

Flexibility as a Strategic Advantage

lexibility is often regarded as a hallmark of strength, yet in the world of real estate investment, it is much more than just a virtue; it is an essential strategy. Investors are frequently confronted with unexpected challenges, from fluctuations in the market to changes in tenant dynamics, regulatory shifts, and even global events that can upheave the economic landscape. Those who develop a mindset of flexibility are better positioned to navigate these challenges and pivot their strategies accordingly. Adapting to circumstances can often mean the difference between success and failure. In this subchapter, we will explore the art of flexibility and how adaptive strategies can not only mitigate risks but also create unforeseen opportunities. Through the stories of various investors who faced seemingly insurmountable obstacles but managed to turn their setbacks into triumphs, we will illustrate that the ability to pivot is not just a skill; it is a strategic advantage.Let's begin with the story of Maria, a young real estate investor who entered the market with high hopes and a well-structured plan. Maria believed that buying and flipping homes in her local market would generate the income she needed to invest in larger properties. She spent months researching neighborhoods, analyzing properties, and securing her first investment, a modest three-bedroom house in an up-and-coming area. At first, everything seemed to be going according to plan. Maria renovated the home as projected and listed it with a keen sense of optimism. However, after a couple of weeks on the market, the listings began to pile up. Her home was not attracting buyers. The city was experiencing an unexpected economic downturn, leading to a significant drop in property demand. For many investors, this moment would have been disheartening, possibly even paralyzing. But Maria recognized a shift; instead of attempting to wait out the market, she pivoted her strategy. Rather than proceeding with her initial plan to sell, Maria decided to rent the property instead. She quickly adapted her approach, re-evaluating her target market and transforming the home into a desirable rental unit. She invested in unique features that appealed to potential tenants, such as high-quality appliances and flexible leasing options. In just a month, Maria secured reliable renters, allowing her to generate income while the market rebounded. Not only did this pivot save her investment but it also allowed her to build equity over time. Maria's story is a powerful testament to the importance of flexibility. Investors often plan meticulously, outlining each step well ahead of time. However, rigid adherence to a predefined strategy can lead to missed opportunities. Real estate is dynamic, and understanding that adaptability is a necessary strength can empower investors to thrive despite uncertainty. Another compelling story comes from Robert, an investor with a rather different challenge. Robert initially focused on commercial properties, believing they would provide stability and high returns. He successfully acquired a small office building in a burgeoning business district. His calculations suggested that with the anticipated influx of companies moving into the area, he would easily lease out the office space and secure consistent revenue streams. Yet, as fate would have it, a pandemic hit—one that dramatically altered the landscape of commercial real estate. Businesses were forced to adapt to remote work, leaving many office spaces vacant and unused.

Robert faced a daunting reality as prospective tenants dwindled. What could have become a financial disaster turned into an opportunity for growth the moment Robert chose to pivot.Instead of clinging to his original plan and trying desperately to lease the space, Robert researched the changing needs of his target market. He discovered a growing demand for shared workspaces and short-term office rentals among freelancers and remote workers. With this new knowledge, he transformed the commercial property into a co-working hub. By understanding the shifting landscape, Robert embraced a flexible approach and expanded his vision.The renovation was striking, and within weeks, Robert had attracted several businesses and individuals who found value in the collaborative work environment he had created. Not only did he mitigate the risks associated with a vacant building, but he also created a new revenue stream that became more profitable than traditional long-term leases. Robert's ability to pivot in response to shifting circumstances exemplifies the powerful impact of flexibility.Flexibility entails more than merely reacting to unfolding events; it is also about anticipating potential changes and proactively preparing for them. One of the best ways to embrace this proactive flexibility is by continually educating yourself about market trends and the broader economic landscape. This knowledge can help you stay a step ahead and allow you to modify your strategies before you are forced to react.Consider the experience of Linda, an investor who focused on residential rental properties. After years of successful investment, she noticed a shift in her local market—an influx of tech workers and young professionals seeking urban living spaces. This demographic preferred apartments that offered luxury amenities and access to vibrant local culture. Rather than performing routine upgrades on her existing properties, Linda seized the opportunity and began to adapt her portfolio.Recognizing that her current properties wouldn't appeal to the emerging market, she sold her lower-end rental units and reinvested that capital into new multifamily properties in a highly desirable neighborhood. With her new acquisitions, Linda customized the renovations to create modern living spaces and introduced amenities such as gyms, rooftop lounges, and co-working areas. Her foresight and willingness to pivot resulted in a portfolio transformation that not only satisfied market demands but also increased her overall returns. These stories illustrate that flexibility isn't just an adaptive response to challenges; it can also be a proactive strategy that creates new opportunities. Establishing an adaptable mindset requires an understanding of one's market and the courage to let go of established plans in favor of new opportunities. To cultivate this mindset, investors can adopt a few key strategies:1. **Continuous Learning:** The world of real estate is constantly evolving. Attend seminars and workshops, subscribe to industry newsletters, and network with other investors to gather insights and data that can inform your decision-making.2. **Data is Your Friend:** Utilize technology and data analytics to track market trends and identify emerging opportunities. Data can help you anticipate shifts and make informed decisions about when to pivot your strategy.3. **Embrace a Lifestyle of Experimentation:** It's essential to foster a culture where experimenting with new ideas is valued. Whether trying out new property types, exploring different markets, or developing various renovation strategies, allow yourself the freedom to explore fresh perspectives.4. **Develop a Versatile Portfolio:** Diversify your investments across various property types and locations. A versatile portfolio can mitigate risks, ensuring that if one segment faces challenges, other investments can still perform.5. **Network with Other Investors:** Surround yourself with fellow investors who share similar values. Collaborate, share experiences, and learn from one another. Being part of a supportive community can provide guidance and inspiration during challenging times.6. **Maintain a Positive Mindset:** Investing can be emotionally taxing. Cultivating resilience—persevering when faced with setbacks and maintaining a positive outlook—allows you to approach challenges with an open mind and discover creative solutions.Now, let's examine a situation highlighting how flexibility applies to current trends and innovations in technology, particularly in the realm of real estate. As society becomes more digitalized, traditional methods of buying, selling, and managing properties are evolving rapidly. Innovations such as virtual reality tours, blockchain technologies, and artificial intelligence are changing the game for real estate investors and business owners alike. Take Jonathan, for example, an investor who had been operating his rental properties the traditional way—local advertising, in-person showings, and manual lease agreements. As technology began transforming the industry, he quickly realized that he either needed to adapt or risk falling behind. Jonathan invested time in researching technology that could streamline processes and enhance the tenant experience. He adopted virtual walkthroughs to showcase his properties and employed digital tools that allowed prospective tenants to apply online and sign leases electronically. As a result, Jonathan not only reached a broader audience but also simplified the application process, making it easier for potential tenants to interact with him. This shift enabled Jonathan to fill vacancies faster and alleviate some of the demands associated with property management. The increased efficiency and convenience he offered attracted high-quality tenants who appreciated modern, tech-savvy management. Jonathan's ability to embrace flexibility and adapt to technological changes solidified his position in the market and provided him with a competitive edge. The beauty of flexibility—as illustrated through these varied experiences—is that it allows investors to harness unpredictability and turn obstacles into opportunities. Each investor, like Maria, Robert, Linda, and Jonathan, teaches us that the path to success is rarely linear. Instead, it is filled with twists and turns, challenges, and chance encounters. Developing the courage to pivot, recognizing when to embrace change, and nurturing an adaptable mindset can help create not just mere survival in turbulent times but robust growth—even in the face of adversity. The real estate landscape will inevitably continue to change. Investors who can navigate these changes with grace, courage, and a flexible mindset will emerge not only as survivors but as savvy opportunists. Embrace the art of flexibility as a strategic advantage and watch as you transform setbacks into stepping stones towards greater success.

Understanding Market Signals

Understanding Market SignalsIn the vast and ever-evolving world of real estate, understanding market signals is akin to possessing a compass that guides you through uncharted waters. Every investor, whether novice or seasoned, must grasp the factors influencing real estate markets to navigate their investment journey effectively. This subchapter will delve into the essential elements of market signals, equipping you with the knowledge needed to adjust your strategies in real-time, ensuring your resilience in the face of challenges.Market signals are the indicators that provide insight into the current health and trajectory of the real estate economy. These signals can reveal opportunities for investment or warn of impending downturns. For aspiring investors, learning to identify and interpret these signals is crucial. It can determine not only the timing of your investments but also the type of properties that will yield the best return on investment.To start, let's discuss the foundational types of market signals: economic indicators, demographic trends, and property-specific signals. Each of these facets contributes to a comprehensive understanding of your market's dynamics. Economic indicators are perhaps the most vital for any investor. Factors such as employment rates, inflation, interest rates, and GDP growth can provide a macro view of the economic environment in which you are operating. For example, when unemployment rates are low, consumer confidence tends to be high. This scenario often leads to an increase in home-buying activity as individuals feel more secure in their financial situations. Conversely, high unemployment rates can indicate a cooling housing market as potential buyers may hesitate to make long-term financial commitments.Another critical economic indicator to monitor is the interest rate set by the Federal Reserve. Changes in interest rates have direct implications on borrowing costs. A rise in rates could push potential homebuyers out of the market, leading to stagnation or even a decline in home prices. For real estate investors, understanding these signals helps assess when to hold, buy, or divest properties. Demographic trends also play a pivotal role in shaping the real estate landscape. Understanding who your buyers or tenants are can dramatically influence your investment decisions. Analyzing population growth, age distribution, and migration patterns can unearth potential opportunities. For instance, if a city is experiencing an influx of younger professionals, investing in multifamily units or condos may be a strategic move. On the other hand, if an area is seeing a significant aging population, single-family homes that accommodate retirees may become more desirable. Moreover, rising urbanization trends should not be overlooked. As more individuals flock to urban settings for employment opportunities and lifestyle amenities, demand for properties in these areas is likely to rise. Identifying these movements allows you to pivot your strategy, ensuring you remain aligned with market demands. Property-specific signals also warrant your attention. This includes understanding the condition of the property, its location, and market saturation. A property that has been well-maintained in a growing neighborhood is likely to yield a different return than one in a declining area. Key indicators such as days on market, price reductions, and absorption rates offer critical insights. For instance, if properties in a certain area are selling quickly with multiple offers, it may indicate a seller's market, while prolonged listings with frequent price cuts hint at growing buyer caution or oversupply. To effectively interpret these market signals, investors must develop a keen analysis system, leveraging both qualitative and quantitative data. Employing a blend of technology and expertise can furnish you with the insights necessary to inform your decisions. Real estate data platforms can provide valuable information regarding property trends, while local news sources can give insights into upcoming developments or economic shifts. Networking with local real estate professionals can also augment your understanding of market dynamics. Engaging with realtors, developers, and fellow investors can surface anecdotal evidence that statistical analysis alone may not reveal. Seasoned professionals can share their experiences, helping you to glean insights that enhance your strategy.In addition to external signals, maintaining a level of self-awareness is crucial for investors. Acknowledging your biases, past successes and failures, and emotional responses to market fluctuations allows for a more objective analysis of market signals. Recognizing when ego or fear might cloud your judgment can be the difference between a strategic pivot and a misguided leap.The art of understanding market signals lies not only in recognizing when to act but in knowing when to pause. The real estate market can be volatile; trends change, economies shift, and unexpected events can disrupt established patterns. Developing a mindset that embraces flexibility is essential. Just as a seasoned sailor adjusts their sails in response to changing winds, so too must an investor remain agile in their approach. As we pivot from theoretical frameworks to practical applications, let's explore actionable methods for integrating market signals into your investment strategy. Begin by conducting regular assessments of your target areas. Create a data dashboard that synthesizes key economic indicators and demographic trends. Focus on data relevant to your investment thesis, whether that pertains to rental income potential, property appreciation, or market demand.Consider enrolling in real estate investment courses or workshops that emphasize market analysis and signal interpretation. Practical training will enhance your analytical skills, allowing you to interpret data meaningfully. Hands-on experience in case studies where market signals were successfully leveraged can solidify your understanding and empower your decision-making.Engagement in local real estate investment groups can also be invaluable. These forums facilitate discussion surrounding budgetary shifts, market entry strategies, and investment targeting, promoting collaborative learning. Members often share experiences of how they interpreted market signals and adjusted their strategies accordingly, providing enlightenment on real-world applications.Moreover, documenting your investment journey can serve as an essential tool for reflection and growth. Keep a journal or develop a portfolio that outlines the decisions you made in response to market signals. Capture what worked, what didn't, and the reasons behind each decision. This practice will help you hone your instincts and refine your ability to interpret signals accurately over time.Finally, let's address the psychological aspect of navigating market signals. Understanding market dynamics can lead to periods of uncertainty or fear, especially in a fluctuating real estate market. However, investing from a place of faith can provide the resilience needed to forge ahead. Faith in your research, faith in the process, and faith in your ability to pivot are essential components of a successful investment mindset.Each failure encountered on your investment journey is an opportunity to build resilience. Market signals may not always lead you to favorable outcomes, but they fortify your understanding of the market landscape, equipping you with the tools needed to thrive. Embrace setbacks as lessons learned, enabling you to pivot with confidence, transforming disappointments into stepping stones for success. In conclusion, understanding market signals is not just about data; it's about fostering an adaptive mindset and nurturing a forward-looking perspective. By honing your ability to interpret economic indicators, demographic trends, and property-specific signals, you equip yourself with the tools necessary to navigate the complex realm of real estate investing. Your ability to pivot in response to these signals will define your journey, allowing you to transform setbacks into triumphs. The world of real estate is ever-changing, but with faith and resilience, you can position yourself at the forefront of opportunity.

Embracing Change

Embracing ChangeIn the ever-evolving landscape of real estate, change is the only constant. Market fluctuations, economic shifts, and new technologies redefine the terrain daily. As aspiring investors, it's crucial to understand that each change, regardless of how daunting it may seem, carries within it the seeds of opportunity. This subchapter invites you to explore how the act of embracing change can be transformative, urging you to cultivate adaptability and resilience—key traits of successful real estate investors.Consider the story of Jessica, a keen investor who first entered the market in the midst of a booming real estate cycle. With her savings and a solid business plan, she seized the moment and quickly acquired properties. It wasn't long before the market began to shift, leading to unexpected financial stress. Prices decelerated, renters became scarce, and her once-promising investments soon felt like anchors. In her struggle, Jessica faced a critical choice—embrace the shift and pivot her strategy or cling to a fading path that offered little hope.Unlike many who would retreat in fear during these unsettled times, Jessica decided to reevaluate her approach. Committing to continuous learning, she immersed herself in seminars and networking events to understand emerging trends. She began to listen—really listen—to the conversations around her: what tenants were looking for in their environments, how digital marketing was reshaping property visibility, and how sustainability was becoming a deciding factor for buyers and renters alike. Change turned her fear of failure into a catalyst for discovery.Her newfound adaptability led her to pivot from traditional rentals to short-term leasing, leveraging the demand that came with tourism in her area. With each adjustment, Jessica discovered layers to her potential - suggesting that the more we are willing to embrace change, the more doors can open. This realization reshaped her identity as an investor; she became a trendsetter instead of a follower, ultimately increasing her portfolio and profits in ways she had never dreamed.Just as the economy reverberates with cycles— booms and busts—our personal experiences and responses to change will shape our narrative. The value of adaptability cannot be overstated. It involves not just a willingness to change in response to external pressures but also the ability to anticipate those changes and proactively adjust one's strategies. This proactive mindset can give aspiring investors a significant edge in an industry where so much is beyond our control.But how do we cultivate this adaptability? One effective approach is to embrace a learning mindset—seeing every setback as a chance to refine and enhance our knowledge. When the traditional approach fails to yield results, ask yourself: what can I learn from this? Each challenge can serve as a stepping stone towards innovation, provided we choose to inquiry rather than retreat. Moreover, exposure to diverse perspectives is vital. Surrounding yourself with other investors, mentors, and professionals allows you to witness a variety of responses to change. It is in these interactions that you might discover new approaches that resonate with you. Implementing the advice or strategies you admire in others can transform a potentially harrowing situation into a successful venture.Consider the procedural changes introduced by technology: virtual tours, online property management systems, and automated leasing processes have revolutionized how we operate. Yet, these advancements have also exposed gaps in traditional methods and left some investors struggling to keep up. The key to leveraging technology effectively lies in your willingness to adapt your processes. The successful investors are those who have stepped up to engage with new tech instead of shying away. They realize that learning to utilize these tools not only helps them streamline operations but also enhances the experiences of their clients.Adapting to change also involves an element of risk management. While changes can offer new opportunities, they can also present unforeseen challenges. Take John, who invested heavily in a commercial property right before the pandemic hit. Initially, he saw potential in the growing market. However, as businesses faced unprecedented closures, he found himself at a crossroads. Rather than viewing his investments as liabilities, he opted to reimagine the space. John reached out to local tenants and engaged with community leaders to understand their needs better. Through these connections, he discovered a significant demand for shared workspace within his commercial building. With quick thinking and a willingness to pivot, he transformed the unused retail units into co-working spaces, catering to freelancers and small businesses seeking adaptable work environments. This transition not only weathered the storm for John's investment but positioned him as a resourceful player in a market that had drastically shifted.When embracing change, remember the importance of mindfulness. Awareness of your thoughts and emotions during difficult transitions can lead to more effective decision-making. Fear and frustration often cloud our judgment, but harnessing a growth mindset enables us to view obstacles as opportunities. Reflect on not just what is changing but how these changes can align with your core values and long-term vision. Surround yourself with reminders of your "why," the passion that drives your investment journey, and how it relates to the world around you. This connection can become an anchor during tumultuous times.Moreover, keeping a flexible action plan is essential. Investing should not be a rigid process; it should reflect both the internal and external changes you encounter. As you encounter shifts—be they local market trends, economic downturns, or changes in consumer behavior—adjust your plans accordingly. A flexible approach prevents stagnation and fosters creativity, allowing you to seize opportunities that may otherwise have gone unnoticed.Embracing change may also call for self-compassion. In a fast-paced and often demanding environment, it is easy to fall into the trap of self-criticism when facing setbacks. Yet, the intangible growth that comes with each experience is invaluable. Allow yourself time to adjust; recognize that every investor faces hurdles along the way. Acknowledging that you are human—and that mistakes are a part of the journey—can cultivate a supportive internal dialogue, one that encourages exploration rather than paralysis by analysis.Equally important is the power of resilience. Resilience is not merely about bouncing back from failures; it is shaping forward progression. In navigating challenges, resilience forms the backbone of a successful investor's mindset. This quality fosters hope and determination, enabling you to seek innovative paths even in the darkest hours. Remember, your ability to adapt in the face of adversity is what defines your success in real estate—and in life. As we dive deeper into developing resilience through embracing change, we should also consider the power of community. Networking with other investors and industry professionals builds a support system that can be leveraged during times of shift. These connections open up channels for knowledge-sharing, collaboration, and mentorship. Much like Jessica regained momentum by learning from others, your network can become a vital resource in navigating change—offering guidance, inspiration, and partnerships when the path ahead seems clouded. When facing challenges, don't hesitate to seek counsel from mentors who have cultivated their own success amidst change. Their personal stories can provide insight into the struggles and triumphs layered on their journeys. Leverage their experiences to nurture your own strategies, but remember that every investor's path is unique. Assimilate their guidance, yet adapt it to fit your specific situation. As you cultivate your adaptability, immerse yourself in constant innovation. Keep abreast of emerging trends not only in real estate but also in adjacent industries such as technology, finance, and sustainability. The landscape of investing shifts rapidly; thus, outdated practices can quickly become ineffective. Remaining open to innovation and transferability across disciplines increases your chances of identifying successful paths as landscapes change. Finally, consider the notion of personal branding in an ever-changing environment. Your approach to change not only shapes your investments but also your reputation within the real estate community. Building a brand that exemplifies adaptability and resilience can yield both financial and social capital. When you cultivate a dynamic presence that reflects your willingness to embrace change, you attract partnerships, clients, and opportunities aligned with your vision. In conclusion, embracing change is not merely an act of survival; it is a strategic choice that can propel your journey as a real estate investor. By learning to pivot effectively and proactively, you turn challenges into windfalls, setbacks into significant growth opportunities. Through stories of investors like Jessica and John, we clearly see that adaptability is a hallmark of success, emphasizing that resilient hearts and open minds can navigate the often unpredictable world of real estate. As you embark on your investment journey, allow change to teach, inspire, and uplift you. Seize each opportunity to learn, grow, and, ultimately, thrive in every landscape that unfolds before you.

Chapter 8

Fairy Tales of Fortune

Heroic Journeys

In the world of real estate, where the stakes are high and the landscape can shift with the slightest economic breeze, stories of triumph often emerge from the ashes of failure. These are not mere anecdotes; they are heroic journeys that showcase the relentless spirit of those who dared to dream big, face overwhelming odds, and ultimately, transform their setbacks into magnificent comebacks. Overcoming adversity is at the heart of every remarkable story—and in real estate, where fortunes can flourish or dwindle, the ability to navigate these ups and downs is crucial.Consider the story of a young entrepreneur named Lisa, who embarked on her real estate journey with little more than a dream and a meager savings account. Lisa grew up in a modest home, where her parents worked tirelessly to make ends meet. From an early age, she was captivated by stories of wealth and success in the real estate industry. However, her reality was far from glamorous. After completing her degree in finance, Lisa found herself overwhelmed by student loans and a tough job market. Despite the pressures weighing on her, her faith in herself never wavered. Real estate was the light at the end of a dark tunnel for Lisa. Armed with the determination to succeed, she diligently researched the market, learning about investment strategies, property management, and the importance of building relationships within the industry. It wasn't long before she encountered her first failure—a promising investment opportunity that fell through at the last minute. The disappointment was crushing, and many in her circle urged her to reconsider her ambitions. However, Lisa's resilience shone brightly. Drawing strength from her faith and an unwavering belief in her own capabilities, she dusted herself off and began exploring alternative opportunities.Months of hard work paid off when Lisa discovered a small, dilapidated property in a burgeoning neighborhood. It was a risk—a significant financial investment for a first-time buyer—but Lisa saw potential where others saw despair. She leveraged her creativity, rolled up her sleeves, and began renovations on the property, often working long nights and weekends. The renovation process was fraught with challenges; she faced delays, unexpected costs, and setbacks. Yet each challenge became a stepping stone rather than a stumbling block. Lisa's determination fueled her vision, and each nail hammered, each wall painted, and each obstacle overcome solidified her conviction. When she finally completed the renovation, the property shone anew, effortlessly merging charm and modernity. What once was an eyesore became a much-coveted home for a young family. After listing it on the market, Lisa was amazed by the response. The property received multiple offers, rapidly escalating in value as the neighborhood continued its transformation. With a hefty profit in hand, Lisa didn't take her earnings and run. Instead, she reinvested in additional properties, utilizing the knowledge gained from her experience. With every new acquisition, Lisa became more adept at identifying value, navigating financing options, and cultivating relationships. Today, she stands as a pillar within her community, empowering others with her story and sharing her insights. Lisa's journey encapsulates the essence of resilience, showcasing how unwavering faith and hard work can elevate individuals from humble   beginnings   to   heights   they   previously   considered unattainable.Another inspiring tale comes from Marcus and his partner, who started their real estate investment journey after years of working in corporate jobs. They were not your typical entrepreneurs; instead, they were diligent professionals who witnessed the intriguing dynamics of the housing market from the sidelines. Marcus had always found comfort in routines, but the idea of trading stability for the unpredictability of real estate was exhilarating. A chance encounter with a local developer became the catalyst for their leap into the unknown.Initially, the duo faced daunting challenges—a fluctuating market, high property prices, and lack of industry connections. Their first foray into real estate was a modest fixer-upper, purchased with little knowledge and a ton of hope. However, they quickly realized they had bitten off more than they could chew. The renovations were riddled with issues, and when it came time to sell, they watched in horror as their profits dwindled. Instead of surrendering to defeat, Marcus and his partner decided to learn from their experiences. They actively sought mentorship, networking with seasoned investors who had navigated similar pitfalls. They immersed themselves in educational resources, absorbing knowledge about property valuation, market trends, and even property law. With newfound insights, they returned to the market, this time armed with a transformative mindset.Their subsequent project—a four-unit apartment building—was transformative not just for their financial situation but for their approach to investments. Instead of relying solely on luck and intuition, they implemented data-driven methodologies and strategic planning. Each decision was carefully calculated, and their efforts paid off handsomely. With keen market awareness, they optimally positioned their property for rental, yielding steady income and allowing for reinvestment into future projects. Marcus's story is one of growth—a testament to the belief that setbacks do not signify failure but rather an invitation to learn and adapt. As their portfolio widened, so did their influence in the community. They practiced ethical real estate investing, focusing on creating affordable housing options that positively impacted their neighborhood. Their commitment to giving back fueled their motivation, proving that success is not merely defined by wealth, but also by the ability to uplift others along the way. As we journey through these tales, we glimpse the essence of what it means to be a resilient real estate investor. The path to success is seldom linear, and each story reveals the intricate tapestry of challenges, lessons, and triumphs. Another remarkable narrative belongs to Daniel, who, after experiencing the loss of both his investment property and his job, found himself at a crossroads. Faced with the dual blow of financial insecurity and emotional turmoil, Daniel could have easily succumbed to despair. Instead, he chose to embrace the chaos as a turning point in his life. With unwavering faith, Daniel sought the stories of others who had weathered storms of their own. Through extensive networking, he discovered a community of investors who shared insights and strategies. Inspired by their resilience and fortitude, he shifted his mindset from one of defeat to one of opportunity. He delved into the world of real estate wholesaling, where he could connect buyers and sellers without the heavy burden of financial investment. Through tenacity and resourcefulness, Daniel developed a keen eye for distressed properties, connecting sellers eager to offload their burdens with buyers ready to invest. His first transaction was small, but it ignited a spark within him. As he gained experience, Daniel honed his skills, cultivating relationships that turned into partnerships and mentorship opportunities. Daniel's journey stands as a reminder that sometimes, the most profound lessons come from the ashes of what once was. His ability to pivot and find creative solutions not only rebuilt his confidence but also led to sustainable success. Today, Daniel serves as a mentor and coach, sharing his insights with others who are eager to enter the real estate arena. His path illustrates the principle that reinvention is possible, and through faith and action, new opportunities can emerge from the shadows of failure. As we celebrate these heroic journeys, it becomes apparent that the heart of real estate investing lies not solely in financial gains, but in the profound personal growth that occurs along the way. Each of these investors entered the market with dreams of financial success; however, what they ultimately discovered was much more valuable—the indomitable spirit of resilience and the ability to inspire others through their experiences. These journeys resonate deeply, reminding aspiring investors that every setback can be reframed as a moment of growth. As you navigate your own path in the real estate landscape, allow the stories of Lisa, Marcus, and Daniel to serve as guiding lights. Their unwavering faith, hard work, and essence of community connection paint a vivid picture of what is possible. When faced with adversity, take a page from their books: embrace the challenges, lean into your support network, and recognize that each failure is a stepping stone towards success. Let us also revisit the broader implications of these heroic journeys. In an industry where narratives and reputations often shape outcomes, the stories we tell ourselves can transform our perspectives. They remind us to redefine failure—not as an end, but as part of the process. By recognizing the value in setbacks, we empower ourselves to approach each challenge with curiosity and creativity. As you embark on your own real estate adventure, hold fast to the belief that your journey can mirror these heroic narratives. Remember the importance of faith, both in yourself and in the possibilities that exist beyond your current circumstances. Seek mentorship, invest in your growth, and surround yourself with a community that uplifts and inspires. Each tale serves as evidence that with tenacity and determination, even the most daunting hurdles can be surmounted. Whether you are just beginning your real estate journey or you are well-worn with experience, take heart in the knowledge that countless others have walk-these trenches before you. Let their narratives fuel your passion, encourage your boldness, and remind you that you hold the power to shape your own story— a story that celebrates resilience, transformation, and ultimately, fortune.

From Rags to Riches

In the realm of real estate, the narratives that emerge often resemble the colorful tales of fairy tales, complete with insurmountable challenges and miraculous triumphs. Yet, unlike fairy tales, the stories within this industry are grounded in reality, demonstrating that setbacks can indeed lead to resounding successes. This subchapter, "From Rags to Riches," unveils the transformative journeys of investors who faced dire circumstances and, through grit and determination, transforming their lives and fortunes.As we delve into these inspiring tales, it's essential to recognize that each investor's story is a testament to the power of faith and resilience. The individuals who will feature in this subchapter faced unique challenges—ranging from financial ruin to personal hardships—yet they emerged on the other side, not just unscathed but thriving, showcasing what is possible in the world of real estate.Our first story centers around Sarah, who, at the age of thirty, confronted a formidable financial setback. Despite being raised in a family that emphasized hard work and perseverance, Sarah found herself in a precarious situation. The dot-com bubble had burst, wiping out her savings as her tech startup faltered. Suddenly, she was left with mounting debt and little more than a dream to start anew. With her back against the wall, Sarah began exploring real estate, intrigued by the notion that property investments could provide a steady income stream. However, with her limited resources, buying a property seemed like an unattainable dream. Yet, she remembered her late grandmother's advice: "Every great fortune begins with a single step." Armed with a small inheritance left to her—a meager sum but significant to her—she took that very step.Without much capital, Sarah turned to creative financing options. She meticulously researched owner financing, a method in which the property seller directly finances the buyer's purchase. After many painstaking weekends of looking for potential leads, she finally stumbled upon an old duplex in a less-desirable neighborhood. The seller, equally burdened by his circumstances, was open to her proposal. Sarah was able to negotiate terms that would allow her to pay off the property gradually, all while living in one unit and renting out the other. Though this initial investment was fraught with challenges—dealing with unreliable tenants, managing repairs, and confronting her own self-doubt—Sarah cultivated resilience. She sought mentorship, connecting with local real estate groups while tirelessly learning the ropes. Each small victory, each tenant payment received, was a validation that her strategy was working.As she became more experienced, Sarah began to form a network of other investors. Inspired by the stories of those who had succeeded before her, she began applying new techniques to scale her investments. Over the next decade, she expanded her portfolio, acquiring multiple properties across the city. Her diligence paid off, and ultimately, she transitioned from a position of financial instability to one of remarkable success, building a multi-million dollar portfolio. Sarah's journey from rags to riches is not merely a fairy tale—it is a testament to the realities faced by many aspiring investors. Her story reminds us that resilience, creativity, and a willingness to learn can lead you through the darkest of times.Next, we delve into the experience of Marcus, whose story illustrates how personal failure can lead to professional redemption. Once a prominent corporate leader in a major financial institution, Marcus faced a public scandal that forced him to resign. The fallout was devastating. In a matter of months, he lost his job, reputation, and much of his savings. Faced with humiliation and uncertainty, Marcus had to find a new path forward. Unsure where to begin, he turned to real estate, an industry he had only ever viewed from the sidelines. With the residual bitterness of his fall from grace still fresh in his heart, Marcus embarked on a journey of redemption. He knew he needed to start small, so he poured his efforts into understanding the basics of the market. He attended workshops, immersed himself in books, and began networking relentlessly. Marcus vividly recalls the moment he closed his first deal: a rundown single-family home in a transitioning neighborhood. With limited funds, he leaned heavily on his vision. The home needed extensive renovations, but he saw potential where others saw problems. Most importantly, he recognized that rejuvenating that property could not only restore his sense of worth but also refine his business acumen. Through relentless hard work, he transformed the property, both structurally and financially. Once it was ready, he rented it out, turning his initial investment into a steady cash flow. This process became Marcus's lifeline; as he gained confidence, he moved on to bigger projects—flipping houses and ultimately diving into multifamily units. His decisive, hands-on approach and his knack for understanding market trends allowed him to scale his investments significantly. Within five years, Marcus not only retrieved his lost fortune but also rebuilt a brand-new identity—a brand rooted in genuine integrity and success in the world of real estate. Marcus's narrative conveys an essential theme: the potential for success exists even in the aftermath of failure. The foundation upon which he built his new life was constructed not merely through financial gain but also through the fortitude that only arises from confronting one's shortcomings.Now we explore the journey of Lisa, who began her investment career as a single mother with a meager income working multiple low-wage jobs. She had always dreamt of real estate but never thought it was feasible given her circumstances. After a particularly challenging year, however, she felt a profound desire for change. Lisa had lived paycheck to paycheck, often worrying about providing for her children's future. One day, while cleaning houses for extra income, a friend encouraged her to consider investing in real estate. At first, the idea seemed absurd; she barely had enough to make ends meet. However, after a few sleepless nights and relentless soul-searching, she committed to pursuing this new challenge.With tenacity, she began researching and absorbing everything she could about real estate investing. She attended seminars, listened to podcasts, and consumed countless books, learning about financing options designed for people in her situation. By creating budgets, cutting unnecessary expenses, and leveraging her existing network, she managed to save enough for a down payment on a small property. Though the first property was daunting, Lisa approached it with the same fearlessness she imparted to her children. She poured her heart into transforming that small home, improving it, not only for rental income but also to instill a sense of pride. As she rented it out, Lisa realized she had not only provided financial stability but an opportunity for her children to witness perseverance as a catalyst for change. Her efforts led to more properties, and Lisa's portfolio grew. Beyond financial independence, her journey created a ripple effect, as her story inspired other single parents in her community, who, like her, dreamed of a better life free from the confining walls of their past. In the tapestry of real estate investing, Lisa's journey exemplifies the profound effect resilience can have on a person's life trajectory. Through faith in herself and the determination to overcome her situation, she transformed her dreams into reality, creating a legacy that would ripple through generations. As we gather these narratives, it's evident that the common thread binding them is resilience. Each investor faced dire circumstances that could easily have led them to abandon their dreams. Yet, what sets them apart is their unwavering resolve to harness their failures and reshape their futures. Our next inspiring tale is the story of Alex, who faced the harrowing collapse of the housing market. A seasoned investor at the time, Alex had built a considerable portfolio enjoying the fruits of a thriving real estate market. However, when the crisis hit, he quickly found himself in a dire situation as values plummeted and properties entered foreclosure at an alarming rate. The challenges were immense— outraged creditors, tarnished credit scores, and a looming sense of despair. It would have been easy for Alex to succumb to defeat, but instead, he turned inward to reassess his approach. He focused on the lessons learned from his mistakes rather than allowing them to haunt him. From that point forward, rather than rushing into decisions based solely on market trends, Alex embarked on a deep learning journey. He made it his mission to seek out undervalued properties that held potential, regardless of the initial price. He cultivated relationships with other investors, lending his expertise while also gaining insights from their experiences.His persistence paid off when he found a neighborhood ripe for revival. While others remained hesitant to invest, Alex saw potential where others saw impending failure. He focused on buy-and-hold strategies rather than quick flips, allowing him to ride the market's recovery. Today, Alex's portfolio reflects the essence of resilience—not a mere financial number, but a thriving testament to the importance of patience and learning through adversity. His journey underscores the reality that sometimes, the greatest successes are born not from avoiding failure but from embracing and learning from it.In their transformed lives, these stories echo the sentiment that success in real estate is not reserved for the privileged few, but is attainable by those willing to forge their own paths through struggle, determination, and faith. It's a journey that transforms not only finances but the very essence of who these individuals are—resilient, brave, and unwavering in their pursuits.We conclude with the tale of Tom and Jessica, a couple who faced the daunting challenge of foreclosure on their home during an economic downturn. Stripped of their circumstances and forced to reevaluate their lives, they decided to turn their misfortune into an opportunity. With limited resources, they took a calculated risk and dived into the world of real estate. Understanding their experience of hardship, they connected with others in similar positions seeking to make their mark. They realized they could not only uplift themselves but also help others in their community who faced similar difficulties.By sharing their experiences and providing guidance, Tom and Jessica became catalysts for change in their area, helping others facing foreclosure translate their struggles into success through the power of real estate investing.Their journey, colored by shared sacrifice, hardship, and ultimately triumph, serves as a microcosm of the resilience necessary in the world of real estate. They embody the belief that every setback can be a setup for a greater comeback—a promise that with faith, understanding, and a strong connection to others, anyone can navigate the trenches of life toward success.In each of these narratives, it becomes evident that the key to success in real estate is not merely tactical knowledge or strategic planning; rather, it is the mindset of unwavering faith, resilience, and an insatiable desire to learn from every experience. Turning failures into stepping stones is not simply a skill but an art—the art of navigating the complexities of life through the lens of determination and hope. These transformative tales serve as beacons of inspiration, reminding us that the rags-to-riches stories we often admire are not just fairy tales. They are realities waiting to be written by those bold enough to take the first step, regardless of their starting point. Whether embarking on this journey from a place of despair or standing at the precipice of failure, like the numerous investors before us, let the threads of resilience and faith weave a new narrative, one that transcends hardships and celebrates the power of human spirit to overcome.

Lessons from Legends

In the world of real estate investing, the tales of legendary investors resonate like the chords of a timeless melody. They are not just stories of fortune but narratives of tenacity, vision, and a relentless pursuit of dreams. These legends have faced setbacks that would daunt most, yet they emerged triumphantly, transforming their failures into stepping stones for success. Their journeys offer crucial lessons that aspiring investors can distill and apply to their investment strategies. This subchapter endeavors to draw key insights from the wealth of experiences that renowned investors have generously shared, providing readers with actionable wisdom to navigate their paths. Consider the story of Donald Bren, a prominent figure in the commercial real estate sector and owner of the Irvine Company. Bren's journey as an investor is a classic story of resilience and foresight. He began his career in the construction business in the 1950s and soon transitioned into real estate development. Bren faced significant challenges early on, including market downturns and opposition from local communities. However, his ability to adapt and his deep understanding of market dynamics enabled him to pivot in times of crisis. One of the key lessons from Bren's story is the importance of understanding the macroeconomic factors that influence real estate markets. Investors should cultivate a keen awareness of market trends, demographic shifts, and economic indicators. By doing so, they can make informed decisions that anticipate market changes rather than react to them.Another tale that merits attention is that of Barbara Corcoran, a legendary real estate mogul and one of the iconic investors on the television show "Shark Tank." Corcoran's journey began with modest means; she started her first real estate company with a mere $1,000 loan. However, what sets Corcoran apart is her resilience in the face of rejection. Throughout her career, she encountered countless setbacks, including the 2008 financial crisis that challenged her real estate empire. Yet, instead of succumbing to despair, Corcoran used each setback as an opportunity to reassess her strategies and innovate. From her experience, aspiring investors can derive a vital lesson: embrace failure as part of the learning curve. Each obstacle presents an opportunity to refine your approach, ask the right questions, and ultimately emerge stronger and more knowledgeable.As we delve deeper into the realm of real estate investment legends, the story of Robert Kiyosaki emerges as a beacon of financial literacy and entrepreneurial spirit. The author of the best-selling book "Rich Dad Poor Dad," Kiyosaki emphasizes the critical role of education in wealth-building. His insights underline that while traditional education may excel, financial education is equally vital. Kiyosaki's discussions about cash flow, assets versus liabilities, and the power of investing in oneself provide essential takeaways for any investor. He advocates for financial education as a pathway not only to understanding real estate but to grasping the intricacies of money flow and wealth generation. Aspiring investors should take heed: cultivating financial literacy and seeking resources—be it through books, seminars, or mentorship—can significantly elevate their investment game.Shifting focus to another legendary figure, we encounter Sam Zell, an influential real estate entrepreneur known for his contrarian investment style and sharp negotiating skills. Zell's experience during the 2008 recession allowed him to refine his approach to risk management. He understood that downturns could often present unique opportunities to acquire undervalued assets. Zell's perspective teaches us the importance of maintaining a level head amid market volatility. For investors, this translates into the ability to conduct thorough research, seize opportunities during market lows, and not be swayed by fear-driven decision-making. By maintaining a balanced view and aligning investment strategies with long-term visions rather than short-term chaos, investors can position themselves to thrive in fluctuating environments.Similarly, the insights of real estate mogul, Gary Keller, co-founder of Keller Williams Realty, resonate deeply with his perspective on goal-setting and productivity. Keller emphasizes the importance of focusing on "one thing" that will yield the most significant results. His philosophy underlines the necessity of prioritization in the hustle and bustle of real estate investing. Too often, newcomers become overwhelmed by the multitude of opportunities that real estate presents, which can lead to analysis paralysis. Keller's advice encourages aspiring investors to hone in on their goals, determining what actions will most effectively drive them toward their desired outcomes. This concentrated approach enables clarity of purpose, reduces distractions, and enhances productivity. In a world filled with noise, finding that one central focus can be a game-changer.Then we must consider the compelling narrative of Grant Cardone, a current heavyweight in the real estate investment arena known for his aggressive investment strategies and motivational prowess. Cardone emphasizes the principle of taking massive action. According to him, the most significant barrier to success is not a lack of opportunity but the hesitation that stems from fear. In his books and talks, he advocates for setting ambitious goals and pursuing them relentlessly. He candidly shares his own mistakes, reinforcing the imperative to learn from missteps while not allowing them to stifle ambition. Cardone's philosophy encourages investors to cultivate confidence and take calculated risks. Aspiring investors should remember that inaction often results in missed opportunities. The lesson here is clear: lean into discomfort, take bold steps, and foster an entrepreneurial mindset that embraces risk.Examining the contributions from these legends not only provides tactical insights into success but also promotes a broader understanding of the mindset required for enduring achievement. Equally important is the understanding that mindset and emotional resilience play pivotal roles in overcoming failures. Invest in your mental fortitude as much as your financial portfolio. The journey of investing is undoubtedly fraught with challenges, and how one responds to those challenges fundamentally shapes the trajectory of their success.In culmination, it becomes evident that the stories of legendary real estate investors embody various principles from which aspiring investors can extract invaluable lessons. Whether it's understanding market dynamics from Donald Bren, embracing failure like Barbara Corcoran, prioritizing education as advocated by Robert Kiyosaki, maintaining a balanced perspective like Sam Zell, honing in on clear objectives a la Gary Keller, or prioritizing action as emphasized by Grant Cardone, each narrative contains golden nuggets of wisdom. Navigating the world of real estate investing doesn't require a crystal ball, but a mindful approach grounded in the insights of those who have walked the path before us. These lessons remind us that failure is not a destiny but a stepping stone—an opportunity to refine our skills and strategies continually. Aspiring investors must remain open to learning, both from the successes and missteps of others, actively incorporating those lessons into their unique journeys. By internalizing these teachings and integrating them into their investment approaches, readers can cultivate resilience, sharpen their insights, and enhance their capacity to turn setbacks into triumphs. Just as the legends unearthed their fortunes from the trenches of hardship, so too can today's aspiring investors emerge victorious through a steadfast commitment to learning and an unwavering belief in the journey of real estate investing.

Chapter 9

THE ZEN OF WAITING

The Art of Patience

In the fast-paced world of real estate, the notion of patience might seem counterintuitive. We live in an age where everything insists on speed: instant messaging, rapid transactions, and social media updates create a culture that celebrates immediacy. This relentless push for quick results can often distort our perception of success and the necessary steps to achieve it. However, as anyone who has navigated the trenches of real estate investing knows, those who learn to embrace patience often find themselves in the most advantageous positions. The art of patience is not merely about waiting; it's about cultivating an understanding of timing and opportunity. It's also about embracing the pauses in the journey, recognizing that each seemingly stagnant moment is actually ripe with potential. As a visionary investor, I've encountered numerous scenarios where the cultivation of patience proved pivotal to achieving long-term success. The lessons derived from these experiences can offer valuable insights into how aspiring real estate investors can transform their mindsets to not only bolster their decision-making but also empower them to thrive in a challenging environment. The first step in mastering the art of patience is understanding its role within the framework of real estate investments. Traditionally thought of as a domain driven by rapid decisions and swift transactions, real estate often requires a counterintuitive approach. Recognizing that not every opportunity demands immediate action can be liberating. In fact, some of the best deals arise from opportunities where one has taken the time to understand the market dynamics, analyze trends, and cultivate relationships with key stakeholders.Consider the story of a client I worked with early in my career. Eager to make a name in the real estate sector, he rushed into his first investment without thorough research or a comprehensive plan. While his enthusiasm was admirable, it ultimately backfired. The property he purchased was in a neighborhood designated for future development, but the transformations were expected to take years. Instead of waiting for the market to mature, he sold his investment for a loss, unaware of the potential gains that could have been awaiting him had he exercised patience.This narrative encapsulates a prevalent theme in real estate: the importance of timing. Each market has its ebbs and flows, and while it can be tempting to jump in during moments of apparent opportunity, true strategic investing often requires a more tempered approach. The right moment might demand waiting—not just for prices to stabilize, but for various external factors to align perfectly, guaranteeing a more fruitful outcome.The process of developing patience starts with a shift in mindset. It's integral for aspiring investors to foster a perspective that views delays as opportunities for growth rather than hindrances to success. To accomplish this, one must routinely practice reflection and evaluation. Instead of focusing solely on the end goal, immersing oneself in the learning process can transform waiting into a period of rich development.Engaging with market analyses, attending seminars, and honing negotiation skills are some of the productive ways to fill the time that could otherwise be spent in anxiety over a deal not closing. This proactive approach lays the groundwork for informed decision-making when the right opportunity presents itself. During these pauses, remember that cultivating expertise creates a reservoir of resilience that can withstand the failures that accompany any investment venture. Thus, how can one cultivate this mindset? The following strategies can serve as stepping stones toward developing a more patient approach to investing. First, identify your long-term vision. What does success look like for you in the realm of real estate? Crafting a clear vision enables you to set goals that align with your ultimate objectives, making the waiting periods feel less like vacuums and more like parts of a larger journey. This vision will also help you differentiate between fleeting opportunities and those that truly warrant your attention.Second, cultivate a support network. Surrounding yourself with like-minded individuals who embrace a patient approach can be immensely valuable. Their insights and shared experiences will reinforce your understanding that in the world of real estate, quick wins are often temporary, while strategic moves foster lasting gains. Engaging with mentors can also significantly enhance this journey; they can share wisdom that comes only from years of experience.Third, keep learning. As markets evolve, so too should your understanding of them. Market conditions can shift dramatically, and those who commit to being lifelong learners are often the ones who identify trends early and act decisively when the time is right. Allocate time each week to read industry reports, watch webinars, or participate in discussions. This not only builds knowledge but enhances confidence in your ability to act when opportunities arise.Additionally, practice mindfulness. The ability to be present can ease the anxiety often associated with waiting and uncertainty. Techniques such as meditation can help ground your thoughts, making it easier to remain calm and composed in the face of delays. A focused mind is more adept at discerning valuable insights and recognizing the right moment to act.Analogous to the seasons of nature, the market has its own cycles. Just as waiting for spring before planting seeds ensures a bountiful harvest, understanding when to invest takes careful observation and intuition. The market will not always serve up opportunities on a silver platter, and there will be moments where you must sit back, observe, and assess. The importance of timing cannot be understated in real estate investing. There are numerous anecdotes within the industry where an investor's willingness to hold or wait for the right moment transformed a potential loss into a substantial gain. Many seasoned investors emphasize the significance of patience, drawing parallels to various forms of art, where the best results often manifest from waiting for the perfect moment to add the final brushstroke. As a case in point, a close colleague once recounted his experience with a rundown property located in a transitioning neighborhood. Initially, the market simply wasn't favorable; values were stagnant, and opportunities for growth felt limited. Rather than letting impatience lead to a hasty decision, he chose to wait. During that time, he focused on building relationships with local developers and understanding emerging trends. This research ultimately revealed that a new transport link was set to open, fundamentally changing the economic landscape of the area. By capitalizing on this knowledge, he could acquire the property just before the anticipated spike in demand. The investment translated into remarkable profit, proving that waiting—while often uncomfortable—can yield extraordinary returns. The third key element in this journey is learning to embrace the discomfort that accompanies patience. In a culture where gratification is sought after, it's easy to perceive waiting as suffering. However, reframing this discomfort can lead to a transformative experience. Instead of viewing it as a negative, consider it a period of character building. The ability to tolerate discomfort can strengthen your resolve as an investor, enhancing your capacity to remain calm during the inevitable storms that arise within the market. Investors often encounter setbacks and challenges that can tempt them to deviate from their strategic plans. In those moments, patience becomes not just a virtue but a survival skill. Understanding that the landscape of real estate is rife with uncertainties allows you to accept the inevitability of setbacks without immediate despair. Each challenge faced is a lesson learned, shaping the investor you will become. Another vital component of practicing patience in real estate is maintaining a close connection with your motivation. Reflecting on why you chose to pursue this path can rekindle your passion during the waits and delays. Documenting your journey in a journal can help clarify these motivations and provide inspiration when faced with frustrations. Regularly revisiting your objectives can provide a sense of reassurance that the fruits of your labor are worth the wait. While patience is indeed an essential trait of successful investors, it should not be mistaken for passivity. The difference lies in how one approaches waiting. Active patience involves continued engagement with the market, identifying opportunities while remaining ready to pounce when the time is right. It's a proactive state of mind that welcomes the folds of time without succumbing to the dreaded paralysis of over-analysis. Moreover, part of exercising patience can involve discerning when to step away. If your instincts tell you something isn't aligning, or if you are simply feeling an overwhelming burden, stepping back can provide clarity. It's essential to create space for reflective thought, as lingering pressure can cloud judgment and lead to rash decisions. Investing is often filled with stories of triumph against adversity, but it's vital to acknowledge that the most successful stories are interspersed with moments of struggle, waiting, and learning. Each setback provides a chance to reassess, recalibrate, and return stronger, equipped with knowledge that hasty decisions often overlook. In conclusion, the art of patience is an indispensable skill in the world of real estate investment. It requires dedication, self-reflection, and a commitment to fostering a resilient mindset. Embracing the quiet moments, investing in learning, and maintaining a steady focus on the long-term vision will pave the way for ultimately achieving success. As you navigate your journey as an aspiring real estate investor, remember that patience is not merely a waiting game, but an art form that, when mastered, can lead to extraordinary opportunities. Let the stories of those who have walked this path before you inspire your strategic approach. Their journeys affirm that the wait can very well be the precursor to your greatest successes, ensuring that your path to fortune is not merely a sprint, but a fulfilling marathon marked by intentional pauses, thoughtful decisions, and enduring faith in the vision you create.

Finding Peace in Uncertainty

The world of real estate is fraught with uncertainty. For every seasoned investor, there comes a moment when the waiting becomes almost unbearable. Perhaps you've submitted an offer on a property but are left hanging, anxiously checking your email for a response. Or maybe you're scouting out a neighborhood, feeling the weight of indecision as you ponder whether the market conditions are right for a purchase. In these moments, the uncertainty can feel like an insurmountable weight, leading to anxiety and self-doubt.But what if I told you that this waiting period could be transformed into a time of peace and productivity? The ability to find peace in uncertainty is not only beneficial to your mental health; it can also significantly enhance your decision-making abilities. In the following pages, we will explore mindfulness techniques that can help you navigate this anxious waiting period. Additionally, we will share inspiring stories of investors who, faced with uncertainty, not only maintained their composure but leveraged that calm to create opportunities for success.At the heart of finding peace in uncertainty lies the practice of mindfulness. Mindfulness can be defined as the state of being present and fully engaged in the current moment. It encourages us to detach from the turbulent thoughts that often accompany uncertainty and instinctively pull us toward worry. This practice is not about suppressing your feelings of anxiety or frustration; rather, it's about observing those feelings without judgment and allowing them to pass through you. Recognizing that uncertainty is a part of the investment journey allows us to accept it as a natural phase rather than an obstacle.One effective mindfulness technique is the practice of deep breathing. When you find yourself caught in a swirl of anxious thoughts, take a moment to breathe deeply. Inhale slowly through your nose, allowing your abdomen to expand fully, and then exhale through your mouth, releasing any tension with the breath. This simple yet powerful exercise can trigger a relaxation response in your body, alleviating feelings of anxiety. Even a couple of minutes of focused deep breathing can help clarify your thoughts and bring you back to a sense of calm.Another helpful practice is the use of mindful observation. Find a quiet place where you can spend a few moments in solitude. As you sit, focus on your surroundings. What do you see? What do you hear? What do you feel? Allow yourself to be fully immersed in these observations. This practice serves as a reminder of the beauty of the present moment and can greatly reduce feelings of anxiety related to uncertainty. Engaging your senses helps pull you out of the cycle of worry, enabling you to approach the waiting game with a fresh perspective.Visualization is also a massively potent tool when navigating through periods of uncertainty. Take a moment to conjure up an image of what you hope to achieve with your investment. Picture the properties you dream of owning or the successful deals you wish to close. Visualizing these outcomes in vivid detail can instill a sense of hope and optimism, shifting your mindset from one of anxiety to one that anticipates possibility. The practice of visualization reinforces your goals and dreams, reminding you to maintain faith in your journey even when the outcome remains unseen.In addition to these mindfulness techniques, drawing inspiration from those who have successfully navigated uncertainty can provide valuable insights and motivation. Consider the story of Jane, a commercial real estate investor who faced a pivotal moment when the market seemed to be in freefall. After spending months scouring for the perfect property, she finally found one that met her criteria. However, just as she was ready to make an offer, news broke of an economic downturn that sent anxiety rippling through the investment community. Friends and colleagues urged her to hold off, citing the uncertain market conditions as a reason to hesitate.Rather than succumbing to the mounting pressure to wait, Jane leaned into her practices of mindfulness. She took time to breathe deeply, allowing the initial anxiety to pass through her. She also engaged in mindful observation, reflecting on the fundamentals of her investment strategy and drawing comfort from the knowledge she had developed over the years. When she visualized her success, she recognized that this property had long-term potential that outweighed the immediate market fluctuations. With her faith in the process restored, Jane made her offer and secured the property, which ultimately became a highlight of her portfolio. The narrative of Jane exemplifies how maintaining a sense of calm during periods of uncertainty can lead to groundbreaking success. Her ability to remain grounded in the moment—a commitment to her mindfulness practice—allowed her to discern opportunity within chaos. Instead of being paralyzed by fear or anxiety, she transformed uncertainty into a calculated decision rooted in faith. Another inspiring example comes from Mark, a real estate wholesaler who, after working tirelessly to secure a deal, found himself facing a prolonged waiting game. After numerous negotiations, he had put in an offer on a home that seemed certain. Then came the silence. Days turned into weeks without a response, and the anxiety began to creep in. Instead of dwelling on the internal turmoil that uncertainty can cause, Mark turned to meditation. He dedicated time to visualize not just the outcome of his offer, but the entire journey of his real estate career. Each day, he would sit quietly, envisioning himself successfully building a thriving network of investments. Eventually, Mark received a call indicating that his offer had been accepted! His perseverance during the waiting period not only solidified this particular deal but also refined his mindset for future investments. By utilizing mindfulness practices, Mark learned that uncertainty can come hand in hand with great opportunity. As we can see from these stories, finding peace amid uncertainty is not always an easy pursuit. It requires patience and dedication to the practices that help ground us. But as you build your own toolkit of mindfulness techniques, remember that every moment spent waiting can also be a moment of preparation for your next success. The process of waiting can cultivate resilience and mental fortitude that will serve you well throughout your investment journey. When the anxiety surfaces, do not shy away from it. Instead, engage with it. Allow it to inform your understanding while holding steadfast to your faith in the process. Recognize that the waiting isn't an absence of action; it's a time for reflection, preparation, and growth.Moreover, learning to embrace uncertainty as an integral part of the investment journey can create pathways to unforeseen success. It's about adopting a mindset that seeks curiosity rather than fear. Uncertainty forces us to evaluate our strategies, challenge our assumptions, and innovate in unexpected ways. As you navigate the waiting period, ask yourself: What can this time teach me? How can I use this waiting to grow in my knowledge and skills?As you embody this mindset of curiosity, opportunities may present themselves that you may not have recognized in a more frantic state. A seemingly idle moment could give birth to a brilliant idea, a pivot in your strategy, or an insight that leads you to the right investment at the right time. When you embrace uncertainty, you empower yourself to reshape the narrative, transforming anxiety into anticipation.In practicing mindfulness and adopting a guiding principle of curiosity, you create a conducive environment for your mind and spirit to thrive amidst uncertainty. Here are a few closing techniques to reinforce your practice:1. **Gratitude Journaling**: Each day, write down three things for which you are grateful related to your investment journey. This practice shifts the focus from anxiety to appreciation, helping to cultivate a positive mindset.2. **Affirmations**: Create simple affirmations related to your investment goals and repeat them daily. For example, "I embrace uncertainty as a pathway to my success" or, "I trust the process of my investment journey." Affirmations reinforce your faith and bolster resilience.3. **Daily Reflection**: Spend a few minutes each evening reflecting on the day. Consider what went well and what you learned from any challenging moments. This practice cultivates an attitude of continuous learning and helps to reduce the weight of uncertainty.4. **Community Conversations**: Share your feelings about uncertainty with a group of fellow investors. Engaging in open dialogue can build camaraderie and provide insights that create trust within the community while alleviating individual anxieties.5. **Mindfulness Walks**: Take time to step outside and go for a walk. During this time, focus intently on the sounds of nature, the feel of the ground beneath your feet, and the rhythm of your breath. Physical movement partnered with mindfulness can provide a powerful soothing effect for anxious thoughts.Finding peace in uncertainty is a skill that cultivates resilience, creativity, and growth during challenging times. By adopting mindfulness techniques and creating a sense of community, you can dismantle the anxiety that uncertainty often brings, replacing it with a serene confidence that will serve you well as you navigate the ever-changing landscape of real estate investment.As you apply these practices to your life, remember that the journey involves movement—progress is never linear, and each experience, including moments of waiting and uncertainty, adds value along the way. Embrace it all. You've got this.

Chapter 10

MANIFESTING DREAMS

Visioning Your Success

Visualization is more than just a buzzword in personal development; it's a powerful technique that can fundamentally change the way you perceive your future and, in turn, the actions you take to achieve it. In the realm of real estate investing, where setbacks are common and challenges abound, a clear and compelling vision can be a game-changer. When you can visualize your success, you create a mental roadmap that keeps you motivated, focused, and driven, especially when the going gets tough.In this subchapter, we will explore various visualization exercises designed to help you craft that vivid picture of your future success. We will draw inspiration from the stories of 'The Resilient Newcomer,' a fictitious character who embodies the struggles and triumphs of many real estate investors embarking on their journey. Through their testimonials, we will see how harnessing the power of visualization can propel you toward excellence.To begin, let's consider the essence of visualization. At its core, it is a cognitive exercise that involves creating mental images of desired outcomes. This process engages your imagination and can evoke emotions tied to achieving these outcomes.

Research shows that visualization can enhance motivation, boost confidence, and increase performance in various domains, including business and athletics. However, it's not just about seeing your success in your mind; it's about feeling it, believing in it, and understanding the steps you need to take to realize it.As we dive into the visualization exercises, it's beneficial to set up your space. Find a quiet, comfortable spot where you can sit or lie down without distractions. You may want to close your eyes, take a few deep breaths to center yourself, and allow your mind to become calm and focused. The exercises that follow will guide you to explore your aspirations, confront your fears, and ultimately picture the success you desire in your real estate ventures.The first exercise focuses on defining your ultimate real estate success. This clarity is essential as it informs your visualization process. Think about what success means to you. For some, it may be financial freedom, while for others, it could be creating sustainable housing in their communities or being a recognized leader in the industry. Join 'The Resilient Newcomer' as they reflect on their vision. They once struggled to articulate their dreams, unsure of what they wanted to achieve in the competitive real estate market. But one day, sitting in their small apartment, they closed their eyes and envisioned a life where they had the leading role in a groundbreaking project—a community-focused housing development that not only provided homes but also uplifted the neighborhood economically and socially.Focus now on what you saw in that vision. Picture the buildings, the smiling faces of families moving in, the vibrant community life flourishing around you. Take a moment to feel the emotions associated with this success: the pride, the joy, the sense of accomplishment. The more details you can incorporate into this image, the clearer your mental picture will become. Write these details down. Make a vision board if you feel inspired to do so, allowing visual references to ground you in your aspirations.As you continue to refine your vision, we will explore the second visualization exercise: the creation of a success timeline. Imagine yourself standing at the beginning of a long, winding road. This journey represents your path in real estate investment. Visualize the milestones you need to reach along the way, including educational pursuits, networking opportunities, projects you want to undertake, and any financial goals you wish to achieve. 'The Resilient Newcomer' recalls a pivotal experience. They visualized their timeline and set specific goals: attending a local real estate seminar within three months, investing in their first property within six months, and earning a steady rental income within a year. This structured vision allowed them to navigate their path with clarity and purpose. You, too, can create markers along your road. Picture reaching out to mentors, acquiring knowledge about property management, exploring financing options, and making informed decisions with confidence. Next, focus on overcoming obstacles along your journey. Visualization works wonders when it comes to building resilience and preparing for challenges. Imagine encountering setbacks—perhaps a deal falls through, a property underperforms, or a mentor is unavailable when you need guidance. Visualize yourself facing these hurdles with poise and toughness. Recall how 'The Resilient Newcomer' pressed forward in the face of difficulties. They embraced failures as learning opportunities, adjusting their strategies accordingly. In your mind, picture the solutions you will explore, the alternative routes you can take, and the support systems you will leverage during tough times. This mental rehearsal reduces anxiety and equips you to react proactively when challenges arise. The next exercise focuses on embodying your vision of success. Picture yourself in the midst of achieving your goals. Imagine the day you acquire your first investment property. Visualize the excitement of negotiating the contract, the sense of fulfillment as you hold the keys and walk through the front door for the first time. Take note of the sights, sounds, and emotions connected to this moment. Allow the thrill of accomplishment and contentment to wash over you. Remember the words of 'The Resilient Newcomer' as they reflect on standing in that property, knowing that every difficult lesson learned paved the way for this achievement. Feel how the weight of past struggles transforms into a sense of pride. As you live this imagined experience, consider how you will maintain that success. Envision yourself attending networking events, mentoring others, and making a positive impact in your community. Picture yourself confidently standing in front of a crowd, sharing your journey and inspiring others with your story of resilience. Breathe in the moment and acknowledge the growth that led you to this point. The power of visualization lies not only in imagining the finish line but also in crafting your role in the ongoing narrative of success. Visualization goes hand-in-hand with affirmation. As part of our journey, let's integrate the practice of affirmations into your visualization exercise. Define positive affirmations that reinforce your vision. Use present-tense statements that resonate with your aspirations, such as "I am a successful real estate investor," or "I attract profitable opportunities with ease." Repeat these affirmations as you visualize your future success. The more you affirm your vision both through imagery and positive statements, the more you program your mind to seek out the resources and opportunities that align with your goals. 'The Resilient Newcomer' would rise each morning, standing in front of a mirror to recite their affirmations, taking note of how their confidence grew over time. They recounted how this practice reoriented their mindset, helping them overcome self-doubt and feel empowered in their pursuits. In this space of affirmation, allow those words to resonate deeply within you, creating a strong foundation for your success. Throughout this subchapter, we have explored multiple dimensions of visualization that pave the way for manifesting your dreams in real estate. Remember that this journey is ongoing. As you grow and evolve, so too should your visions. Regularly revisit your visualization exercises, adapting them as needed and enhancing your mental imagery. Create a powerful, dynamic blueprint of your success that reflects your change and growth. As we conclude this exploration of visualization, consider how it interweaves with faith and resilience. Faith is the unwavering belief in your capabilities, even in uncertain circumstances, while resilience enables you to bounce back from failures and setbacks. Together, these principles form the backbone of effective visualization. By imagining your success, affirming it, and preparing for challenges, you cultivate the faith necessary to pursue your aspirations wholeheartedly.Harness the power of your imagination, grounded in the rich stories of fellow investors like 'The Resilient Newcomer.' Let their experiences inspire and empower you to craft your unique vision. As you move forward in your journey as a real estate investor, remember that success starts with a thought, a vision, and the unyielding belief that you can transform your dreams into reality. Take the time today to close your eyes, breathe deeply, and visualize the incredible future that awaits you.

Action Steps Toward Manifestation

In the journey of manifesting dreams, it is essential to transform aspirations into actionable steps. The vision that exists in your mind is the first spark of creation, but it is through action that those dreams become tangible. This subchapter will delve into specific strategies that will help you align your passions with your goals, infusing your path forward with the energy needed to propel you into success. To begin with, self-reflection is key. Take a moment to envision where you see yourself in the next five to ten years. Picture the life you want to lead, the properties you wish to invest in, and the impact you desire to make in your community. Write this vision down in vivid detail. What does your ideal day look like? Who are the people you interact with? How do you feel? This practice of visualization aligns your subconscious with your conscious goals, acting as a powerful catalyst for manifestation.As you create a clear picture of your future, establish specific, achievable goals. The SMART (Specific, Measurable, Achievable, Relevant, Time-bound) criteria serve as an excellent framework for goal-setting. For instance, instead of saying, "I want to invest in real estate," reframe that to, "I want to purchase my first rental property within the next 12 months, focusing on a two-bedroom apartment in my preferred neighborhood." This precision clarifies your path and makes the vision seem more attainable.Following this, break your larger goals down into smaller, manageable tasks. If your goal is to purchase a property within the year, outline the steps needed to make that happen. This might include researching neighborhoods, securing financing, attending seminars, and networking with other investors. Create a timeline for these tasks, assigning due dates to keep yourself accountable. Incorporating motivational quotes can invigorate this process, providing you with consistent reminders of your capabilities. For instance, consider the words of Winston Churchill: "Success is not final, failure is not fatal: It is the courage to continue that counts." These affirmations remind us that every setback is merely a stepping stone on the path to success. Another action step involves the incorporation of daily affirmations. These powerful declarations can shape your mindset and reinforce your commitment to your goals. Begin each day with a set of affirmations that resonate with you, perhaps something like: "I am capable of achieving all my dreams," or "Each step I take brings me closer to my goals." By embedding these positive statements into your daily routine, you reinforce a mindset of resilience and purpose.Moreover, cultivate a supportive environment. Surround yourself with like-minded individuals who are also pursuing their dreams. This network will not only keep you motivated but can provide invaluable resources and insights. Attend local real estate meetups, join online forums, and connect with mentors in the industry. As you share your goals with others, you also invite accountability—people who will check in on your progress, celebrate your successes, and encourage you during challenging times.Community support can be further enhanced by finding an accountability partner. This person should understand your goals and be willing to discuss progress, brainstorm solutions, and celebrate milestones. Establish regular check-ins, whether they be weekly or bi-weekly, to create a structured space for reflection and growth. An accountability partner turns the solitary endeavor of achieving your dreams into a shared journey, one that is marked by mutual support and motivation.Additionally, embrace the concept of 'learning through failure.'

Remember that fear of failure often holds people back from taking essential actions. Instead of viewing missteps as failures, consider them as essential learning experiences. Each setback carries valuable lessons that can help redirect your path toward success. Reflect on past challenges you've encountered, and analyze how they've shaped your current perspective. As the writer C.S. Lewis once said, "Failures, repeated failures, are finger posts on the road to achievement." To further enhance your learning process, commit to continuous education. The real estate industry is continually evolving, with new trends and techniques emerging regularly. Dedicate time to read books, listen to podcasts, and take online courses related to real estate investing. Knowledge not only empowers you but builds your confidence, equipping you to make informed decisions on your journey. In building out your strategic plan, don't forget to engage in self-care and mindfulness practices. Maintaining mental and emotional health is crucial for sustained focus and success. Incorporate activities that replenish your energy and enhance your well-being, such as regular exercise, meditation, or journaling. Cultivating a sense of balance helps to prevent burnout and keeps your enthusiasm intact.As you take on these action steps, celebrate your progress along the way. Establish a reward system for completing tasks or reaching milestones. Rewards serve as a positive reinforcement that fuels motivation and reminds you of the joy inherent in pursuing your dreams. Each accomplishment, no matter how small, deserves recognition. Establish a 'Victory Log' where you document every win—this will serve as a powerful reminder of your capabilities and progress, even during tough times.Mindfulness and gratitude practices can be beneficial as well. Each week, take a moment to reflect on what you're grateful for in your life and endeavors. Gratitude shifts your focus from what is lacking to what is present, promoting a positive mindset that nurtures success. In tandem with these strategies, consider creating a vision board. This tool can serve as both a source of inspiration and a visual reminder of your goals. Cut out images, quotes, and symbols that resonate with your vision, and arrange them in a way that is visually appealing to you. Place your vision board somewhere you'll see it daily, reinforcing your aspirations and keeping your goals at the forefront of your mind.As you manifest your dreams, remember the importance of faith. Faith in your vision, in your capabilities, and the belief that you are deserving of success is vital. As Nelson Mandela said, "It always seems impossible until it's done." Let the strength of your passion be your guiding star, steering you toward your ultimate destination.Finally, don't hesitate to revisit and adjust your goals and action plans. The journey of manifesting dreams is not static; it evolves as you grow. Regularly assess your progress and be flexible in your approach. This adaptability allows you to navigate obstacles while staying aligned with your true passions and aspirations.Manifesting your dreams is not merely about wishing or hoping; it requires intentional action, unwavering belief, and a willingness to learn and grow. By following these actionable strategies, you empower yourself to translate your visions into reality, aligning your goals with your passions. As you persist through challenges, let the fuel of motivation—quotes, affirmations, community support, and a commitment to learning—guide you toward the fulfillment of your dreams.In the world of real estate investing, where the road can be particularly rocky, the act of manifesting requires boldness and resilience. Finally, never underestimate the power of consistency. Small, daily actions lead to monumental changes over time. Trust the process, remain committed, and watch as your dreams come to life.

Staying Committed to Your Vision

In the realm of real estate investment, the path to success is often laden with obstacles, uncertainties, and setbacks. However, the cornerstone of turning visions into reality is commitment. Staying committed to your vision is not merely a passive endeavor; it is an active, sometimes tumultuous journey marked by trials and triumphs. This subchapter aims to emphasize the unwavering resolve required to breathe life into dreams, weaving together the inspiring tales of individuals who have exhibited remarkable perseverance against daunting odds. Throughout history, countless stories emerge of individuals who desired something greater. They faced challenges that would make most people falter, yet they pressed on, fueled by an unshakeable commitment to their vision. Their journeys can serve as a beacon of hope and inspiration for anyone navigating the uncertain waters of real estate. Consider the story of Sarah, a woman whose dreams in real estate began with a simple desire: to provide affordable housing in her community. Raised in a neighborhood plagued by economic hardship, she understood all too well the struggles faced by her neighbors. With little savings and no formal education in real estate, Sarah's dream teetered on the verge of impossibility. Yet, she remained steadfast in her commitment. She spent countless hours reading books on property management, attending workshops, and networking with established investors. Her commitment was tested when, after saving for years, she finally acquired her first property—a dilapidated building that needed extensive renovations. Many around her expressed doubts, urging her to sell and cut her losses, but Sarah's unwavering belief in her vision kept her grounded. She rolled up her sleeves, taking on the renovations herself, learning from every setback and honing her skills. With each brush stroke and hammer knock, she was not just rebuilding a structure; she was constructing her future. Her commitment allowed her to turn that neglected property into a thriving rental space, providing homes for many families in need. Sarah's story is a testament to the power of commitment. It illustrates that unwavering perseverance transforms obstacles into stepping stones toward success. The energy and determination required to overcome each challenge is crucial for any aspiring real estate investor. Every setback, whether it be financial struggles, market downturns, or personal crises, can either serve to deter or motivate. The question, then, is how one cultivates that unwavering commitment. The first step is to forge a clear vision. This vision must be compelling enough to inspire action even when the going gets tough. It must resonate deeply, rooted in personal values and the desire to make a difference. A vision anchored in purpose can become a guiding light, illuminating the darkest pathways and reminding investors why they embarked on this journey in the first place. It can act as a balm against discouragement, allowing individuals to see beyond their current struggles.Yet, commitment isn't just about being steadfast in a single vision. It's also about adaptability. Real estate markets can shift rapidly, and what once seemed like a promising investment can turn sour. This is where the stories of resilience shine brightest. Take, for example, the tale of Marcus, who ventured into the commercial real estate sector during a period of economic instability. Initially, he struggled to fill vacancies in his properties as businesses folded and consumer confidence waned. Many in his circle advised him to pivot his investments or abandon the sector altogether.However, Marcus recognized that true commitment often requires flexibility. Instead of abandoning his vision, he adapted it. He began seeking out start-ups looking for affordable office space and partnered with local businesses to create a vibrant community hub—an idea that served both his tenants and his investment. This commitment to aligning his vision with the evolving market dynamics eventually led to a flourishing portfolio, proving that steadfastness can coexist with adaptability. A crucial part of remaining committed to a vision is surrounding oneself with a support system. Mentor relationships can prove invaluable. Seek out individuals who have traveled the path before you, who understand the ups and downs of the journey. Their experiences can serve as mere anecdotes or, more importantly, as lessons that resonate with the challenges you face. Mentorship embodies the spirit of community in the real estate world; it fosters a culture of shared knowledge, bolstering one another through trials.In addition to mentorship, accountability plays a significant role in sustaining commitment. Sharing your goals with others creates a network of responsibility that can motivate you when the energy to press on wanes. Consider the story of Lila, an aspiring investor who formed a mastermind group with fellow real estate enthusiasts. Together, they would set quarterly goals, celebrate each other's successes, and hold one another accountable during challenging times. When Lila faced unexpected financial difficulties, it was her accountability group that pushed her to refine her budgeting strategies and seek creative solutions. Their unwavering support fueled her perseverance, keeping her on track to achieve her vision. While commitment is often associated with a single goal, it is essential to recognize that the journey is often a multi-faceted one. Embracing the beauty of diversifying one's vision can enrich the entire path. For instance, consider Jason, whose commitment to investing in real estate transformed an initial focus on residential properties into a broader interest in sustainable building practices. After attending a conference on eco-friendly construction, Jason's vision evolved. He realized that not only did he want to invest in properties, but he also wanted to play a role in positively impacting the environment. This pivot required an immense amount of learning and recalibrating. Equipped with passion and commitment, Jason immersed himself in understanding sustainable design, renewable resources, and energy-efficient technology. Though there were moments of doubt, he pressed on, and his innovative approach soon attracted clientele eager for sustainable living options. His evolution in vision exemplifies how commitment can intersect with growth, pushing us to expand as we continue our journeys. Moreover, maintaining a growth mindset is fundamental to commitment. Having faith in your abilities and seeing failures as opportunities for learning fuels resilience. Let me share the story of Maria, who faced numerous rejections when she first sought funding for her real estate ventures. Each "no" felt like a crushing blow, yet she treated them as invaluable lessons instead of setbacks. She studied each rejection meticulously, seeking feedback and refining her pitch. This relentless pursuit ultimately attracted the attention of a significant investor who shared her vision. Maria's journey reflects that commitment to learn, adapt, and grow in the case of failure can lead to extraordinary outcomes. As aspiring real estate investors navigate their unique paths, they will inevitably encounter moments of disillusionment. External factors, such as market volatility, can evoke doubt. Nevertheless, it is crucial to harness a deep-seated faith in one's vision and capabilities. This commitment is not synonymous with rigidity; rather, it requires a solidarity of purpose amid fluctuations. Even the most successful investors often encounter scenarios that challenge their beliefs, but those who emerge victorious are those who remain undeterred.Consider the inspiring words of an iconic real estate mogul, who once stated, "Success consists of going from failure to failure without loss of enthusiasm." This perspective encapsulates the essence of staying committed to your vision. When you embody a commitment steered by passion, purpose, and resilience, you not only develop the ability to weather storms but also cultivate the tenacity to thrive in them.Equally important in the journey of commitment is the recognition that success is rarely an overnight phenomenon. The path is long and often winding. Just as Sarah invested years into her vision and Marcus adapted through struggle, so must aspiring investors be prepared for the long haul. The investments they make—of time, effort, and emotion— will not yield results immediately. Remaining committed during the waiting period is one of the most challenging aspects of manifesting dreams.In building commitment, celebrating small victories can be transformative. Each step toward the ultimate goal is a brick laid in the foundation of success. These small achievements, whether acquiring a property, successfully networking, or gaining a new client, should be acknowledged and celebrated. They are the concrete markers of progress, reinforcement for commitment, and reminders that the journey is unfolding.By drawing parallels to their own lives and examining the stories of perseverance, aspiring real estate investors can cultivate the desire to remain committed to their visions. The narratives of Sarah, Marcus, Jason, and Maria illustrate the multifaceted nature of commitment— the ability to adapt, learn, and grow, even in the face of failure.In moments of uncertainty, especially when dreams seem far away, let us glean courage from those who have come before us. Their triumphs are testaments to the human spirit's unruly capacity for resilience. In staying committed, you do not just chase a dream; you forge a pathway, illuminating the way for those who may tread it after you. As you set forth on your own journey through the complex landscape of real estate investment, may you carry the stories of the committed within you. Let them inspire grit in the face of challenging circumstances. May your vision act as your compass, steadfast in the storms, adaptable through the shifting tides of the market. With unwavering faith in your ability to transform setbacks into stepping stones, remember that turning dreams into reality is not simply a destination—it is a lifelong journey of commitment, perseverance, and endurance. In each endeavor, every failure, and every triumph, there lies an opportunity to reaffirm your commitment and to manifest dreams practiced diligently, one determined step at a time.

Chapter 11

An Investor's Lifelong Journey

Continuous Learning and Growth

In the world of real estate investing, the only certainty is change. Markets fluctuate, regulations evolve, and the needs of consumers shift. To thrive amidst this constant flux, one must embrace a mindset of continuous learning and growth. This subchapter seeks to illuminate the paths taken by successful investors, illustrating how their commitment to lifelong education has equipped them to navigate challenges, seize opportunities, and ultimately transform setbacks into triumphs.As we delve into the stories of various real estate tycoons, it is essential to highlight that their journeys were not without hardships. Many faced significant setbacks—economic downturns, failed projects, and harsh criticisms. What sets them apart is their capacity to turn those failures into lessons, driving them to learn more, adapt their strategies, and re-enter the fray with renewed vigor. Their experiences underscore a fundamental truth: the most significant investment one can make is in their own knowledge and skills.Consider the journey of Lisa Torres, a self-made real estate mogul who began her career in a small town, investing in fixer-uppers. Initially, Lisa struggled to navigate the complexities of renovation budgets and market analysis. However, instead of succumbing to frustration, she enrolled in courses focused on property valuation and construction management. These resources not only refined her understanding of the market but also empowered her to make informed decisions that greatly reduced her financial risk.Lisa's story is a prime example of how a proactive approach to learning can yield tangible results. As she began to implement her newfound knowledge, she transformed her investment strategy from trial and error to a systematic approach grounded in research and analysis. Her return on investment began to soar, and soon enough, Lisa was not just flipping homes but successfully managing multiple rental properties and entering commercial real estate. Each stage of her growth was marked by a deliberate choice to seek out knowledge and apply it.Yet, even amid her successes, Lisa recognized that the journey of learning was never truly complete. She became a regular attendee at industry conferences, not merely to acquire new skills, but also to build valuable networks. Those connections allowed her to partner with other investors, share insights, and collaborate on larger projects. In doing so, Lisa illustrates another essential lesson: learning is magnified through collaboration. The exchange of ideas and perspectives can lead to innovative approaches that might not emerge in isolation.The digital age has further revolutionized the pathways to knowledge. Online courses, webinars, and access to countless resources mean that aspiring investors can educate themselves from their own homes. The story of Eric Ramirez exemplifies this trend. A former school teacher turned investor, Eric faced the daunting challenge of transitioning into a field where he had limited experience. However, instead of succumbing to self-doubt, he leveraged technology, immersing himself in podcasts, online tutorials, and virtual mentorship programs.Eric's journey demonstrates how diverse learning channels can enhance one's understanding of complex subjects such as real estate finance and negotiations. What was once overwhelming soon became a series of manageable lessons. He transformed his challenges into a structured learning agenda, focusing each week on a different aspect of investing—from market analysis to tenant relations. This strategy resulted in not only increased confidence but also a well-rounded skill set that allowed him to identify opportunities that others overlooked.Yet, the essence of continuous learning transcends mere accumulation of knowledge. It also involves unlearning—letting go of outdated practices or beliefs that no longer serve a purpose in a rapidly evolving market. Sarah Wu, a seasoned investor with over two decades of experience, shares her own realization of the importance of unlearning. After years of following traditional investment strategies that had worked in stable markets, Sarah found herself struggling when the market dynamics began to shift dramatically. Faced with declining property values and changing tenant preferences, she recognized the need for a new strategy. The first step was acknowledging that some of her long-held beliefs were hindering her ability to adapt. She began exploring emerging trends, embracing technology in property management, and learning about eco-friendly building practices that not only appealed to a trendy consumer base but also attracted premium tenants. By unlearning what she thought she knew, Sarah positioned herself to capitalize on new opportunities and pivot her business model effectively.As we reflect on these stories, it becomes evident that the act of continuous learning is inextricably linked to resilience. Each investor faced unforeseen obstacles, but their determination to grow and adapt empowered them to push through adversity. This synergy between learning and resilience is vital for budding investors. They must approach their endeavors with an eagerness to absorb lessons from both success and failure. The real estate landscape is increasingly competitive, and the most successful investors are those who view every setback as a potential lesson rather than a permanent defeat. Each failure comes with data—an opportunity to evaluate what went wrong and how it can be avoided in the future. Keith Anderson, who experienced his fair share of real estate failures, embodies this philosophy. After a particularly challenging investment project that did not yield the anticipated returns, Keith did not retreat. Instead, he assembled a small group of fellow investors to dissect the project in detail.In their discussions, they analyzed every decision, from financing choices to renovation practices. This collaborative learning experience not only illuminated the mistakes made but also uncovered alternative strategies that could have been employed. Keith's commitment to understanding failure paved the way for greater success in subsequent endeavors as he was able to integrate hard-won lessons into his future investments.Adaptability also warrants continuous education, particularly in areas that might not seem directly related to real estate. Melanie James, another successful investor, underscores the importance of emotional intelligence in her business dealings. Early in her career, Melanie noticed that her negotiations often fell flat, not due to terms or price, but because she overlooked the essential human aspect of her interactions. In response, she chose to immerse herself in courses focusing on interpersonal skills and negotiation tactics.As she honed these skills, Melanie found her approach to investing transformed. Understanding her clients' needs and perspectives led to more effective negotiations, stronger relationships, and, ultimately, a more sustainable business model. In recognizing the need to grow beyond just technical real estate skills, Melanie illustrates how comprehensive learning can yield growth across many dimensions of life—financial and otherwise.For investors, the commitment to learning doesn't end with formal education or self-study. The real estate landscape is always evolving, and staying ahead of trends necessitates ongoing diligence. It can be beneficial for investors to maintain an active presence in industry circles. Following blogs, subscribing to newsletters, and engaging in forums can provide insights that are invaluable in staying informed about new regulations, market trends, and technological innovations. Networking also presents opportunities to learn from the experiences of others—an informal yet powerful method of knowledge sharing.The stories of investors emphasize that being engaged in the community can unveil insights that textbooks may not cover. This continuous exchange of ideas nurtures an environment where investors inspire one another. Regularly attending local networking gatherings or joining professional associations not only sharpens one's skill set but fosters relationships that can prove mutually beneficial.Moreover, the role of mentorship within the context of continuous learning cannot be overstated. The most successful investors often attribute their growth to the guidance of mentors who have already traversed the paths they wish to take. Mentorship provides a unique opportunity to gain perspective and advice from those with more experience, shortening the learning curve significantly.Take Rachel Green, for example, who found a mentor early in her investing career. This connection not only offered guidance through her initial ventures but also facilitated introductions to influential players in the industry. Under her mentor's wing, Rachel learned not only the mechanics of investing but also crucial moments of empathy and human connection that are vital in the business. Her mentor's wisdom allowed her to avoid common pitfalls and navigate challenges with confidence.Combining mentorship with a willingness to give back creates a cycle of learning that enriches the real estate community. Many seasoned investors advocate for aspiring individuals, providing guidance and sharing their journeys in a bid to foster success. This dual role—the learner and the teacher—enhances one's own understanding and establishes a cooperative environment within the industry.Ultimately, continuous learning and growth represent a commitment to transformation and improvement. Whether it is through formal education, practical experience, pursuing mentorship, or engaging with the community, the ongoing quest for knowledge serves as a cornerstone for successful investing. Investors must embrace this journey with the understanding that they will inevitably face failures, yet within those failures lie the seeds of growth.In conclusion, the tales and experiences of prominent investors illustrate that the road to success is paved with ongoing education and adaptability. The market will always present challenges, but those who adopt a mindset of continuous learning will emerge not only more knowledgeable but also more resilient. With faith in oneself and a commitment to improvement, aspiring investors can navigate the trenches of real estate, transforming setbacks into remarkable successes. By fostering an ethos of lifelong learning, they can create sustainable strategies that not only secure financial prosperity but also enrich their journeys as individuals.

Giving Back to the Community

In the vast landscape of real estate investing, success is often measured by financial returns, property acquisitions, and market positioning. However, one of the most profound and often overlooked metrics of success is the impact investors can have on their communities. This segment explores the transformative power of giving back—a reciprocal process that not only uplifts neighborhoods but also enriches the investorial spirit and journey.Investing in real estate is about more than just numbers; it's about people. Every transaction, every block of land, and every building has a story woven into its very structure—stories of families, dreams, struggles, and triumphs. By actively engaging with and giving back to the community, investors can shift narratives, fostering environments where both individuals and businesses thrive. This commitment to community is not just an ethical consideration; it creates tangible ripples of positive change, enhancing both personal fulfillment and long-term investment success.Take, for instance, the story of Linda, an investor in a once-declining neighborhood known for its vibrant history but struggling economy. Linda wasn't just focused on purchasing properties at low costs; she envisioned revitalizing the community. After successfully acquiring several vacant buildings, she embarked on a mission to transform them into affordable housing and commercial spaces. Her investments were paired with outreach programs that aimed at teaching financial literacy to the locals, particularly single mothers striving for stability. Linda shared her own journey of successes and failures in investing, providing mentorship and real-life experiences that grounded her teachings. As a result, not only did she see an increase in her property values, but she also built a network of empowered residents eager to invest in their futures. Linda's journey exemplifies how giving back can lead to an improved community atmosphere that ultimately benefits everyone involved. Her story intertwines faith in that community's potential with resilience in overcoming the obstacles that sometimes arise from challenging property investments. The act of investing thus transformed into a shared journey of growth, establishing connections that extended far beyond the balance sheet. Another powerful testament comes from David, who found himself navigating the hardships of investing during a financial downturn. Frustrated by stagnant property values and tenant turnover, he contemplated leaving the industry. However, through introspection and encouragement from his peers, he redirected his efforts toward uplifting his local community. David discovered many disadvantaged families within his properties who lacked access to resources that could uplift them. Instead of retreating, David organized community clean-up days, which fostered a sense of pride among residents. He initiated workshops with local businesses aimed at enhancing skills and employability among those desperate for work. These small steps culminated in a noticeable change in communal attitude. Neighbors began to take ownership, resulting in better-maintained properties and, eventually, a rise in property values—a testament to the collective effort. The ripple effect of David's initiatives not only helped repair his financial standing but also solidified his role as a community leader. This transformation highlighted the importance of faith in humanity. David learned that through investing in people, investment in properties could flourish organically. The ability to pivot during challenging times, shifting focus toward community empowerment, is a testament to resilience—the very bedrock of not just investing but life itself. Evidence shows that giving back and community engagement can enhance long-term investment outcomes. Investors aligned with their community's needs witness a more profound loyalty from residents and clients. When community members feel valued, the relationship becomes a partnership rather than a transaction. For instance, Sarah, another investor, leveraged her expertise in property management while enhancing education initiatives in her area. She created programs that allowed local youth to learn about real estate, finance, and entrepreneurship. The result was a new generation of informed individuals eager to invest back into their neighborhoods. Sarah's faith in the potential of these young people illustrated a critical point: investing isn't just about the present; it's a legacy for the future. When investors take the time to nurture the aspirations of those around them, they create a lineage of collective success that echoes through generations. The friendships forged through mentorship and shared accountability can lead to collaborative investment ventures and partnerships that multiply impact.Looking at these stories, it becomes increasingly clear that giving back to the community fosters resilience not only within neighborhoods but also within the hearts of investors themselves. Entrepreneurs often prioritize financial accomplishments, yet it's the stories of connection and triumph that sustain their respective journeys—the essence of what it truly means to invest. The interweaving of faith in one's self, faith in the community, and resilience in the face of adversity shapes an investor's lifelong journey.The institutions of faith—whether they be non-profits, churches, or organizations built for community outreach—are vital pillars in this journey of giving back. By partnering with these entities, investors can reach parts of their communities that need support the most. In turn, the investors become active participants in developing solutions for local issues. Tying back to Linda's journey, her partnership with the local church allowed for a community food pantry, which served hundreds of families in need. This collaboration is a prime example of how faith-based organizations can amplify an investor's impact while fostering stronger community bonds.When we talk about faith, it's also essential to address the spiritual aspect of real estate investing. Many investors draw inspiration from their beliefs, fueling their missions to uplift others. In what ways can investors integrate their values and spiritual beliefs into their entrepreneurial endeavors? By examining the principles of compassion, kindness, and service, investors can craft missions that resonate beyond profit margins.Greg is an investor who has embodied this faith-based approach. With a background in social work, Greg's investments have consistently focused on solutions to homelessness and transitional housing. Rather than seeing the homeless population as a problem to be solved, he views them as individuals with potential for rehabilitation and success. His faith encouraged him to form coalitions with local governments and shelters to create housing that caters to those who need it most.Investors like Greg remind us that while financial success is a motivator, a greater purpose can lead to deeper fulfillment. The partnership between profit and purpose becomes inherently intertwined when investors employ their passions and assets to fortify their communities. There's a generational shift occurring in the realm of investing. The advent of social media and digital platforms has revolutionized how investors interact with their communities. Investors now have more opportunities than ever to share their missions and stories, inspiring others to follow suit. Platforms like Instagram or LinkedIn allow these narratives of community service to reach broader audiences, attracting potential partners, investors, and movers of change.For example, Dana realized that sharing her focus on revitalizing local parks led to grants and partnerships with environmental organizations. By utilizing her platform to advocate for green spaces, she fostered community involvement that not only beautified the area but significantly increased property values, benefitting her investments. The blending of social media outreach and community investment is an essential strategy for today's investors, illustrating how giving back can create a cycle of reciprocity.Many investors also engage in Direct Community Investments (DCI), a relatively new approach where funds raised through properties are directly funneled back into the local community. This investment strategy acknowledges that economically healthy communities lead to resilient investors. Initiatives might range from supporting local schools to investing in recreation centers that promote well-being amongst families. Julia, an investor who adopted this model, experienced firsthand the synergy that arises when communities are engaged in the solutions. By allocating a portion of her profits toward initiatives that foster education and economic development, she inspired other investors to rethink how they measure success. What had started as a personal commitment quickly evolved into a movement, encouraging a generation of conscious investors to redefine the standard for community engagement. The profound principle here is that everything comes full circle. The more investors give back, the more they receive—not solely in financial terms but in relationships, trust, and community resilience. The investors who immerse themselves in improved community dynamics often find their own pathways illuminated by the successes of others. Their values of faith and resilience become deeply rooted in the very fabric of all they touch. In conclusion, as investors carve their way through the competitive landscape of real estate, they must remain steadfast in their commitment to uplifting their communities. By embracing the stories, beliefs, and challenges of those around them, investors not only enhance their profitability but also their legacy. The journey of investing becomes a shared experience—one where failures become lessons and successes blossom from communal support. While markets may fluctuate, the spirit of giving back remains a constant, flourishing connection that defines the lifelong journey of an investor. In the end, it is the essence of human connection—our ability to nurture, uplift, and inspire—that creates the most profound transformations. As these narratives of resilience and faith take root, they generate ripples of positive change that resonate far beyond financial gains. Investing becomes a shared endeavor, a tapestry woven with stories of courage, compassion, and unwavering commitment to a better tomorrow. The impact of giving back isn't just felt in the present moment; it leaves an enduring legacy for future generations, and in this way, true success is achieved.

Legacy and Future Aspirations

In the world of real estate investing, each decision, each setback, and each triumph plays a pivotal role in crafting the legacy we leave behind. As you venture through your investing journey, it's essential to take a moment to reflect not only on the outcomes but also on the footprints you leave in this realm. Your legacy is not merely a reflection of wealth accumulated but an embodiment of the values, lessons learned, and the positive impact you have made.Envisioning your legacy begins with understanding the innate connection between your ambitions and your values. What do you stand for? What principles guide you through the inevitable ups and downs? As we navigate the complexities of real estate investing, it's easy to become engulfed in the tangible aspects—like closing deals, managing properties, or analyzing market trends. Yet, beyond these immediate concerns lies a broader vision: the influence and the mark you wish to leave on your community, your family, and the next generation of investors.As individuals, we carry the weight of our experiences, both good and bad. The learning curve in real estate is steep, and through reflection, we can distill these experiences into wisdom. Consider the failures you've encountered along the way. Each misstep, each property that didn't perform as expected, taught you invaluable lessons about resilience and adaptability. Rather than viewing these moments as mere setbacks, see them as foundational stones of your legacy. They reveal your tenacity and serve as testaments to your commitment to growth. What's crucial is how you choose to share these lessons with others, especially those who hope to walk similar paths.Imagine the power of stories that recount not only your victories but also your struggles. The narrative of your journey can inspire others, help them recognize that failure is often a stepping stone towards success. It is through vulnerability in sharing these experiences that you can foster an environment where others feel empowered to take risks. In motivating those around you, you create a ripple effect that has the potential to linger far beyond your lifetime.Moreover, consider the relationships you've built throughout your investing career. Each partnership, mentorship, or connection formed with fellow investors, contractors, and community members contributes another dimension to your legacy. These relationships are not transactional; they are opportunities to uplift others, foster collaboration, and create a community centered around shared success. By investing in relationships, you not only accumulate wealth in a traditional sense but also enrich your community, cultivating a sense of belonging and purpose.Additionally, think about the impact of your investments on the environments and neighborhoods you are involved in. Your choice of properties might influence not only your financial future but also the quality of life for many individuals and families. As an aspiring investor, strive to be a steward of positive change. Consider properties that enhance communities, promote sustainability, and provide affordable housing solutions. When your vision aligns with social responsibility, you create a legacy that resonates deeply with your values and aspirations. This is more than just investment; it is a commitment to making the world a better place.Faith plays an integral role in framing this legacy. Real estate investing requires conviction—a belief in yourself, in your decisions, and in the possibilities that lie ahead. This faith operates in multiple layers: it sustains you through tough times, fuels your aspirations, and ignites your passion to continue pushing boundaries. When you align your faith with your investment approach, it informs your decisions, giving a higher purpose to your plans. Whether it is through charitable contributions, community initiatives, or simply encouraging others to rise, your faith can become a guiding light, illuminating paths for those who look to you for guidance.As you envision your future aspirations, it's crucial to identify specific goals that resonate with your long-term vision. What do you hope to accomplish? Is it aimed at financial independence, creating a family legacy, or perhaps building a framework that nurtures upcoming investors? These aspirations should stem from your values, serving as a compass for your decisions.Map out clear milestones that guide you toward these aspirations. Consider setting targets not only for asset acquisition but also for mentoring others or contributing to the community. How can you measure your success beyond financial metrics? Create a layout of what success looks like for you holistically. This exercise allows you to visualize your legacy in action, bringing clarity and motivation to your everyday investing activities. Don't overlook the continuous nature of this journey. Just as you gather experience and wisdom, ongoing education remains vital. Staying informed about market trends, learning from industry leaders, and engaging with evolving investment strategies should be woven into your legacy-building efforts. Harnessing resources, attending seminars, and being part of investment groups can enhance your knowledge and expand your network. By cultivating a mindset of lifelong learning, you not only increase your investment acumen but also inspire others to do the same, amplifying your legacy within the community of investors.Equally important is the environment you create for future generations. As you gain insights and experience, consider how to effectively communicate this knowledge to those who will come after you. Formal mentoring programs, workshops, or even writing your own materials can serve as tools for nurturing the next wave of investors. The act of training others not only cements your understanding but also extends the life of your legacy, encouraging those who follow to continue the journey of resilience and faith.Within this setting of shared knowledge, don't forget the foundational concept of adaptability. Real estate markets are dynamic; they are influenced by social, economic, and cultural shifts. Your ability to pivot and reassess your strategies in the face of change will define your longevity as an investor. Encouraging those around you to embrace flexibility, fostering a culture of innovation, ensures that your legacy remains relevant and impactful.In conclusion, as you reflect on the legacy you wish to create, consider the stories you want to tell and the influence you want to wield. Transitioning from simply pursuing personal success to imprinting a positive mark on society amplifies the reach of your journey. This journey is about more than just housing; it's about transforming lives, empowering others, and instilling values that outlive our individual pursuits. Your legacy is not just what you accumulate or achieve but who you uplift, what you share, and the change you inspire.As you step forward into future aspirations, remember, you are not alone. Countless others journey alongside you. Embrace collaboration, share your stories, and remind yourself of the invaluable lessons learned through both triumphs and trials. Equip yourself with faith and resilience, and let this serve as your guiding light through the complexities of real estate investing. The power of your legacy is within you—it is yours to shape, to expand, and ultimately, to pass on to those who are ready to rise and walk their own paths.Ultimately, when you look back on your investing journey, may you see a tapestry woven with threads of faith, tenacity, and an unwavering commitment to uplift others. This, truly, is the legacy that will echo long after your final deal is closed. Embrace your position as a legacy builder, and let each choice lead you closer to the future you dream to create.

UNTIL NEXT
TIME, FABULOUS READER!

And here we are at the finish line, my wonderful reader! Wow! What a journey it's been! I hope every chapter embraced you with warmth and sparked a flicker of light in your mind. I'm genuinely grateful for you choosing to accompany me through these pages, lending your thoughts, your time, and your energy. It means the world and makes this whole endeavor worthwhile.

Reflecting on all that we've explored together, I hope you found nuggets of wisdom that resonate with your own life. Just like a tasty recipe for a favorite dish, I believe that the blend of ideas and stories shared within this book can serve as ingredients for personal growth and insight. Never underestimate the power that a single idea can have in igniting your passion or steering your life in a fabulous new direction!

Remember that this isn't the end—it's just the beginning of our ongoing conversation. Take what you've learned and let it simmer, let it stew, and then watch as it blossoms into something incredible in your life. Whether it's applying a new perspective to an old problem or sharing an insight with a friend over coffee, I urge you to keep the dialogue alive. Share the love, share the stories, and spread the knowledge!

So, what's next? I hope you feel encouraged to continue your own journey of self-discovery and exploration after closing this book. Dive into your passions, ask those tough questions, and never stop being curious. The universe is vast, and every step you take can lead you to extraordinary places. No limits, only possibilities!

Thank you once again for being such an integral part of this adventure. Together, let's start a revolution of thought, kindness, and creativity that ripples out into the world. I'm cheering for you, always rooting for your growth and dreams. Until we meet again, keep shining bright!

With sparkling gratitude,
Corey Griffin

ABOUT THE AUTHOR

Corey Levelle Griffin – Born in Joliet, Illinois in 1983 to Gene B Griffin And Darlene R Griffin 3rd child of 5 siblings and raised in Columbus, Georgia, Corey Levelle Griffin is a living example of what relentless determination and vision can achieve. From his early school days in Columbus, Corey was known as a dreamer and a doer—someone who never waited for opportunity but chased it down, even when it meant hearing a thousand "no's" before one "yes."

In 2006, Corey began his professional journey by joining Pipefitters Union Local 52 as an apprentice. Through years of hard work and dedication, he rose to become a United States journeyman pipefitter and certified welder, specializing in nuclear power plant projects across the country. His work in this field earned him respect for his precision, leadership, and commitment to excellence.

But Corey's ambition didn't stop there. With the same drive that fueled his success in skilled trades, he stepped into the world of real estate investing— starting with multiple wholesale deals, then moving into fix-and-flip projects, rental properties, and short-term Airbnb investments. Each step was a lesson, each challenge a stepping stone.

Today, Corey is developing new residential communities across Georgia and Alabama, bringing quality housing and revitalized neighborhoods to life. Alongside his wife Nekiya, he launched CNKG Enterprise LLC on July 17,

2015—a company built on faith, vision, and the belief that generational wealth begins with bold action. Their goal: to expand globally, transforming lives and landscapes through real estate.

Over the years, Corey has cultivated powerful relationships with major players in the real estate sector, partnering with private lenders and commercial banking institutions around the world. His reputation as a trustworthy, forward-thinking entrepreneur continues to open doors that once seemed impossible.

Corey is also a devoted husband, proud father of two, and grandfather to three beautiful grandchildren. His family is his foundation, and his legacy is being built not only through business, but through the values of perseverance, integrity, and purpose.

For more information on finding off market or real estate leads visit the site: www.cgriffinrealestateoffice.com